4TH Edition

BEST TENT
Camping

THE
CAROLINAS

YOUR CAR-CAMPING GUIDE TO SCENIC BEAUTY, THE SOUNDS
OF NATURE, AND AN ESCAPE FROM CIVILIZATION

T0152572

This book is for residents of North Carolina and South Carolina
who enjoy some great places to live, work, and tent camp.

Best Tent Camping: The Carolinas
Copyright © 2019 by Johnny Molloy

All rights reserved
Manufactured in China
Published by Menasha Ridge Press
Distributed by Publishers Group West
Fourth edition, second printing 2020

Library of Congress Cataloging-in-Publication Data
Names: Molloy, Johnny, 1961- author.
Title: Best tent camping. The Carolinas : your car-camping guide to scenic beauty, the sounds of nature, and an escape
    from civilization / Johnny Molloy. Other titles: Carolinas : a guide for car campers who hate RVs, concrete slabs,
    and loud portable stereos
Description: Fourth Edition. | Birmingham, Alabama : Menasha Ridge Press, an imprint of AdventureKEEN, [2019] |
    "This book is for residents of North Carolina and South Carolina who enjoy some great places to live, work, and tent
    camp." | "Distributed by Publishers Group West"—T.p. verso. | Includes index.
Identifiers: LCCN 2018038111| ISBN 9781634041515 (paperback) | ISBN 9781634042918 (ebook)
Subjects: LCSH: Camping—North Carolina—Guidebooks. | Camp sites, facilities, etc.—North Carolina—Guidebooks.
    | North Carolina—Guidebooks. | Camping—South Carolina—Guidebooks. | Camp sites, facilities, etc.—South
    Carolina—Guidebooks. | South Carolina—Guidebooks.
Classification: LCC GV191.42.N2 M65 2019 | DDC 796.540975—dc23
LC record available at https://lccn.loc.gov/2018038111

Cover and book design: Jonathan Norberg
Cover photo: The spillway at Old Levi Mill Lake in Poinsett State Park (campground 45, page 148), © Johnny Molloy;
    inset photo © Guy J. Sagi/Shutterstock
Interior photos by Johnny Molloy unless otherwise noted on page and as follows: page ix: Jon Bilous/Shutterstock;
    page 76: jdwfoto/Shutterstock; page 104: Pi-Lens/Shutterstock; page 136: Jill Lang/Shutterstock
Maps by Steve Jones

MENASHA RIDGE PRESS
An imprint of AdventureKEEN
2204 First Ave. S, Ste. 102
Birmingham, AL 35233
800-443-7227, fax 205-326-1012

Visit menasharidge.com for a complete listing of our books and for ordering information. Contact us at our website, at
facebook.com/menasharidge, or at twitter.com/menasharidge with questions or comments. To find out more about
who we are and what we're doing, visit blog.menasharidge.com.

4TH Edition

BEST TENT
Camping

THE
CAROLINAS

YOUR CAR-CAMPING GUIDE TO SCENIC BEAUTY, THE SOUNDS
OF NATURE, AND AN ESCAPE FROM CIVILIZATION

Johnny Molloy

MENASHA RIDGE PRESS
Your Guide to the Outdoors Since 1982

North Carolina Campground Overview Map

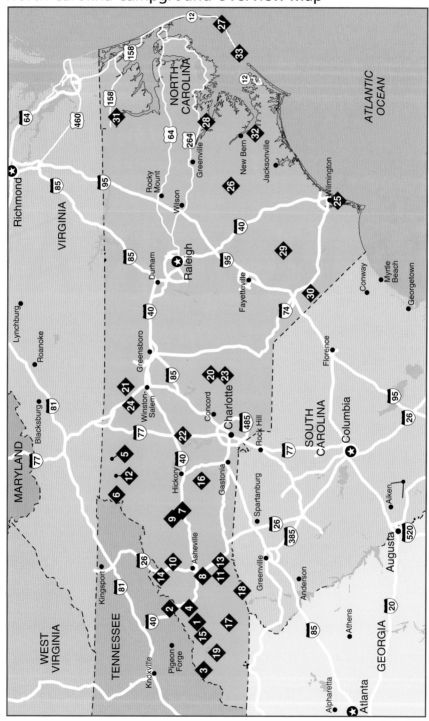

South Carolina Campground Overview Map

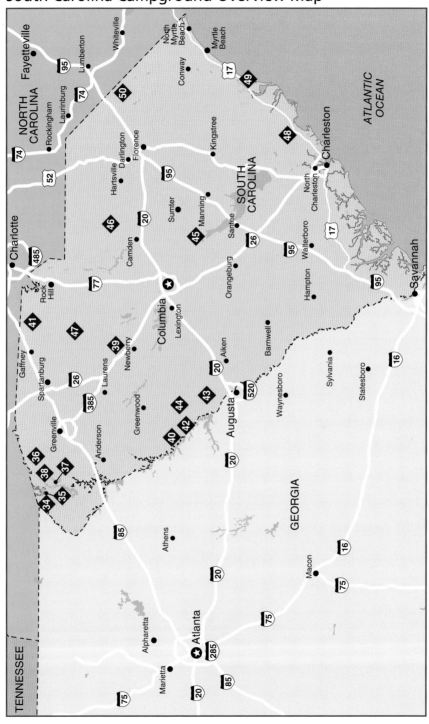

Map Legend

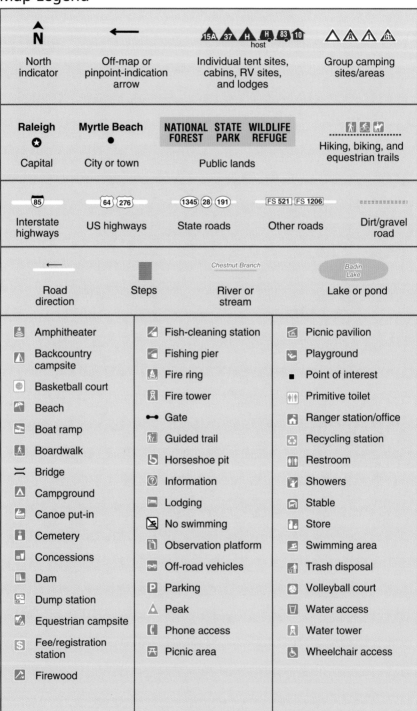

N	North indicator
←	Off-map or pinpoint-indication arrow
	Individual tent sites, cabins, RV sites, and lodges
	Group camping sites/areas

Raleigh ✪	Capital
Myrtle Beach ●	City or town
NATIONAL FOREST **STATE PARK** **WILDLIFE REFUGE**	Public lands
	Hiking, biking, and equestrian trails

85	Interstate highways
64 276	US highways
1345 28 191	State roads
FS 521 FS 1206	Other roads
	Dirt/gravel road

←	Road direction
	Steps
Chestnut Branch	River or stream
Badin Lake	Lake or pond

Amphitheater

Backcountry campsite

Basketball court

Beach

Boat ramp

Boardwalk

Bridge

Campground

Canoe put-in

Cemetery

Concessions

Dam

Dump station

Equestrian campsite

Fee/registration station

Firewood

Fish-cleaning station

Fishing pier

Fire ring

Fire tower

Gate

Guided trail

Horseshoe pit

Information

Lodging

No swimming

Observation platform

Off-road vehicles

Parking

Peak

Phone access

Picnic area

Picnic pavilion

Playground

Point of interest

Primitive toilet

Ranger station/office

Recycling station

Restroom

Showers

Stable

Store

Swimming area

Trash disposal

Volleyball court

Water access

Water tower

Wheelchair access

CONTENTS

NORTH CAROLINA MOUNTAINS 11

NORTH CAROLINA PIEDMONT 69

ACKNOWLEDGMENTS

I would like to thank all of the land managers of North Carolina's and South Carolina's state parks and forests, as well as the folks at the national forests, for helping me in the research and writing of this book. Thanks to Sierra Designs for providing me with a high-quality tent in which to camp, night after night after night.

My biggest thanks of all goes to the people of North Carolina and South Carolina. They have beautiful and historic states in which to tent camp.

An Appalachian vista from the Mount Mitchell observation tower *(see campground 10, page 39)*

PREFACE

As a proud Southerner who believes that our region is the most beautiful in our great country, I jumped at the chance to write *Best Tent Camping: The Carolinas*. And for the fourth edition, I was eager to update the campgrounds in these great states. Having extensively explored the outdoors and written about North and South Carolina, I looked at writing this book as an opportunity to thoroughly and systematically explore the entirety of the two states, via tent camping, of course. With a Sierra Designs tent and laptop in my Jeep, combined with my past experiences, I took off, exploring by day and tent camping at night, breaking out the computer to type up on-site reports about each destination.

My high expectations were exceeded. I knew the islands and beaches were beautiful from past visits, but have you been to the Outer Banks in the fall, with a cool breeze and warm golden light spilling onto its sands? Have you gazed from the top of Mount Mitchell and looked upon the glory of the Southern Appalachians, or sought the distant horizon from the rock monoliths at Table Rock State Park? However, to me, what lay between the Atlantic beaches and the Appalachian range was most surprising.

In North Carolina, Merchants Millpond State Park features a swamp not unlike the famed Okefenokee Swamp of Georgia. The Lumber River also has dark water and is a federally designated wild and scenic river. The Piedmont has the Uwharrie National Forest, where hiking trails wind beneath verdant forested hills broken by clear streams. Pilot Mountain stands where the Piedmont meets the hills, and its cylindrical, flat-topped cone rises 1,400 feet above the surrounding landscape.

In South Carolina, the pleasant surprises start in the Francis Marion National Forest, just a few miles inland from the Atlantic Ocean. This locale offers a long stretch of the Palmetto Trail, a nature study amid wooded wetlands, and canoe routes through some of the least-trammeled terrain in the Palmetto State. Sand Hills State Forest harbors an ecosystem unique to the Carolinas. The varied tracts of the Sumter National Forest in the Midlands offer great recreational opportunities. The Buncombe Trail, now a South Carolina favorite of mine, circles sleepy Brick House Campground. Lick Fork Lake is an ideal mix of campground and land- and water-based recreation in an attractive setting. LeRoys Ferry Campground, operated by the U.S. Army Corps of Engineers, is a quiet respite on big Thurmond Reservoir. And Poinsett State Park is an ecological wonder, with vegetation from the sand hills, the mountains, and the coast, all in one great destination.

Even the mountains offered some new surprises, such as the New River in the northwest corner of North Carolina. This ancient watercourse winds its way through steep hills, offering excellent canoeing and fishing for smallmouth bass. For forays onto the river, use the Wagoner Access Unit of New River State Park as a base camp. Primitive

Honey Hill Recreation Area was my base camp for paddling and hiking the Francis Marion National Forest.

With the aid of the helpful folks at Menasha Ridge Press, this fourth edition, complete with updates, has now come to be. I made many wonderful memories along the way and expect to make many more in the Carolinas. I hope this tent-camping guide will help you make some memories of your own.

—Johnny Molloy

Wild azaleas bloom along the shore of Lake Keowee (*see campground 37, page 123*).

BEST
CAMPGROUNDS

BEST CAMPGROUNDS FOR HIKING

BEST CAMPGROUNDS FOR MOUNTAIN BIKERS

BEST CAMPGROUNDS FOR PADDLING

BEST CAMPGROUNDS FOR FISHING

BEST CAMPGROUNDS FOR WILDLIFE WATCHING

BEST CAMPGROUNDS FOR SOLITUDE

Looking out over the Blue Ridge Mountains from near Mount Pisgah *(see campground 11, page 42)*

BEST CAMPGROUNDS FOR PRIVACY

BEST LAKE CAMPGROUNDS

BEST RIVER/CREEK CAMPGROUNDS

BEST BEACH CAMPGROUNDS

BEST HIGH COUNTRY CAMPGROUNDS

INTRODUCTION

A WORD ABOUT THIS BOOK AND TENT CAMPING

It is a pleasure to introduce the fourth edition of this book. North and South Carolina offer varied and scenic ecosystems, as well as a rich human history. Both states stretch from the alluring Blue Ridge Mountains in the west—the highest, and some would argue, the most scenic range of the Appalachians—to the saltwater-washed sands of the Atlantic coast in the east. The Southern Appalachians, unmatched in biodiversity amid temperate climes, offer shady forests through which clear streams dance over gray boulders, feeding rivers that race toward the Piedmont. Here, where the hills soften, the beauty is more subtle yet clearly alive to the discerning camper. Enhancing this natural charm, many rivers have been impounded to offer the tent camper endless recreation opportunities on the water. The central lands give way to the coastal plain, where dark rivers quietly flow among brooding cypress trees. Moving east, the water of the mountains meets the water of the sea, forming rich estuarine habitats that further complement the ecosystem. Finally, the land ends at the Atlantic Ocean's edge, bordered by slender sand-island chains and shell-dotted beaches.

It is in the Carolinas where much of our country's formative history took place. For starters, did you know that more Revolutionary War battles between the Americans and the British took place in South Carolina than in any other state, or that the first English-speaking colonies in North America were in North Carolina? In fact, under a charter from Queen Elizabeth, Sir Walter Raleigh initiated two North Carolina colonies in the 1580s. It is this melding of human and natural history that makes exploring the Carolinas so appealing.

Today, tent campers can enjoy each of these distinct regions of the Carolinas. At the lofty altitude of 6,320 feet in Mount Mitchell State Park, you can pitch your tent at the highest campground in the East. Or camp along a federally designated Wild and Scenic River, such as the Chattooga or the New. The central Carolinas have quiet Woods Ferry, where Civil War soldiers once crossed the Broad River and where you can rejoin nature at West Morris Mountain. The coastal plain also has scenic rivers ready to be explored, such as the Lumber and the Little Pee Dee. A tent camper has to take a ferry to reach Ocracoke Campground. And there is Frisco Campground, about as far east as you can tent camp in the Carolinas, where tall dunes of sand rise high. All this spells paradise for the tent camper. No matter where you go, the scenery never fails to please the eye.

Before embarking on a trip, take time to prepare. Many of the best tent campgrounds are a fair distance from the civilized world, and you'll want to enjoy yourself rather than make supply or gear runs. Visit campground websites for more information, including maps and regulations. If you can't find a clear answer, call ahead and ask park personnel for other information to help you plan your trip. Make reservations wherever applicable, especially at popular state parks. And don't forget to inquire about the latest reservation and entrance fees at state parks and forests.

Ask questions. Ask more questions. Although this guidebook is an indispensable tool for the Carolina-bound tent camper, the more questions you ask, the fewer surprises you will get. There are other times, however, when you'll grab your gear and this book, hop in the car, and just wing it. This can be an adventure in its own right.

THE RATING SYSTEM

Included in this book is a rating system for the Carolinas' best tent campgrounds. Certain attributes—beauty, site privacy, site spaciousness, quiet, security, and cleanliness and upkeep—are ranked using a star system. Five stars are ideal; one is acceptable. This system will help you find the campground that has the attributes you desire.

★★★★★   The site is **ideal** in that category.

★★★★   The site is **exemplary** in that category.

★★★   The site is **very good** in that category.

★★   The site is **above average** in that category.

★   The site is **acceptable** in that category.

BEAUTY

In the best campgrounds, the fluid shapes and elements of nature—flora, water, land, and sky—meld to create locales that seem tailor-made for tent camping. The best sites are so attractive that you may be tempted not to leave your outdoor home. A little campsite enhancement is necessary to make the scenic area camper-friendly, but too many reminders of civilization have eliminated many a campground from inclusion in this book.

PRIVACY

A little understory foliage goes a long way in making you feel comfortable once you've picked your site for the night. Fortunately, there is a trend toward planting natural borders between campsites if the borders don't already exist. With some trees or brush to define the sites, campers have their own personal space. Then you can go about the pleasures of tent camping without keeping up with the Joneses at the site next door—or them with you.

SPACIOUSNESS

This attribute can be very important, depending on how much of a gearhead you are and the size of your group. Campers with family-style tents and screen shelters need a large, flat spot on which to pitch their tents, and they still have to get to the ice chest to prepare foods, all the while not getting burned near the fire ring. Gearheads need adequate space to show off their portable glow-in-the-dark lounge chairs and other pricey gewgaws to neighbors strolling by. I just want enough room to keep my bedroom, den, and kitchen separate.

QUIET

The music of the lakes, rivers, and all the land between—singing birds, rushing streams, waves lapping against the shoreline, wind whooshing through the trees—includes the kinds of noises tent campers associate with being in the Carolinas. In concert, the sounds of nature camouflage the sounds you don't want to hear, such as autos coming and going or loud neighbors.

SECURITY

Campground security is relative. A remote campground in an undeveloped area is usually safe, but don't tempt potential thieves by leaving your valuables out for all to see. Use common sense and go with your instinct. Campground hosts are wonderful to have around, and state parks with locked gates are ideal for security. Get to know your neighbors and develop a buddy system to watch each other's belongings when possible.

CLEANLINESS

I'm a stickler for this one. Nothing sabotages a scenic campground like trash. Most of the campgrounds in this guidebook are clean. More-rustic campgrounds (my favorites) usually receive less maintenance. Busy weekends and holidays will show the effects; however, don't let a little litter spoil your good time. Help clean up, and think of it as doing your part for the Carolinas' natural environment.

THE OVERVIEW MAPS AND LEGEND

Use the overview maps on pages iv and v to assess the exact location of each campground. The campground's number appears not only on the overview maps but also in the table of contents and on the profile's first page. A map legend that details the symbols found on the campground-layout maps appears on page vi.

CAMPGROUND-LAYOUT MAPS

Each profile contains a detailed campground-layout map that provides an overhead look at campground sites, internal roads, facilities, and other key items.

CAMPGROUND-ENTRANCE GPS COORDINATES

Each profile in this guidebook includes the GPS coordinates for each site entrance. The intersection of the latitude (north) and longitude (west) coordinates orient you at the entrance. Please note that this guidebook uses the degree–decimal minute format for presenting the GPS coordinates. Example:

N35° 33.902'   W83° 10.465'

To convert GPS coordinates from degrees, minutes, and seconds to the above degree–decimal minute format, the seconds are divided by 60. For more on GPS technology, visit usgs.gov.

WEATHER

Weather in the Carolinas is as variable as its elevations, which range from sea level to 6,683 feet at Mount Mitchell. Spring starts in South Carolina's Lowcountry, then works its way northwest across the Piedmont and onward to the Southern Appalachians. Campgrounds in the high country open later. Spring in the mountains can be cool and wet, but by May leaf out reaches the mountaintops. By June, the Carolinas reach the summer season, with accompanying warmth and afternoon thunderstorms. The beaches are best enjoyed in spring and fall, as is the Piedmont. Summer is the time to head for the mountains, to escape the lowland heat. Fall offers cooler temperatures, the least rain of the year, and clear skies. Winter reverses the weather pattern, first coming to the highest elevations and working southeast to the sea. Following the weather patterns of the Carolinas will allow tent campers to enjoy the best weather at the right times.

FIRST AID KIT

A useful first aid kit may contain more items than you might think necessary. These are just the basics. Prepackaged kits in waterproof bags are available. As a preventive measure, take along sunscreen and insect repellent. Even though quite a few items are listed here, they pack down into a small space:

- Adhesive bandages

- Antibiotic ointment

- Antiseptic or disinfectant, such as Betadine or hydrogen peroxide

- Benadryl or the generic equivalent, diphenhydramine (in case of allergic reactions)

- Butterfly-closure bandages

- Comb and tweezers (for removing ticks from your skin)

- Elastic bandages or joint wraps

- Emergency poncho

- Epinephrine in a prefilled syringe (for people known to have severe allergic reactions to such things as bee stings)

- Gauze (one roll and six 4-by-4-inch pads)

- Ibuprofen or acetaminophen

- Insect repellent

- LED flashlight or headlamp

- Matches or pocket lighter

- Mirror for signaling passing aircraft

- Moleskin/Spenco 2nd Skin

- Pocketknife or multipurpose tool

- Sunscreen/lip balm
- Waterproof first aid tape
- Whistle (it's more effective in signaling rescuers than your voice)

FLORA & FAUNA PRECAUTIONS

SNAKES

North Carolina is home to 37 varieties of snakes, 8 of which are venomous: the coral snake, cottonmouth, copperhead, diamondback rattler, pygmy rattler, timber rattler, scarlet snake, and scarlet king snake. South Carolina has three venomous snakes among its varieties: the timber rattler, copperhead, and Eastern diamondback rattler. The first two are found throughout the state, while the last one is found in the coastal plain. A good rule of thumb is to give whatever animal you encounter a wide berth and leave it alone.

TICKS

Ticks like to hang out in the brush that grows along trails. They are common in the woodlands of the Piedmont of North Carolina and Midlands of South Carolina. You should be tick aware during the warm season. The ticks that light onto you while hiking will be very small, sometimes so tiny that you won't be able to spot them. Primarily of two varieties, deer ticks and dog ticks, both need a few hours of actual attachment before they can transmit any disease they may harbor. I've found ticks in my socks and on my legs several hours after a hike that have not yet anchored. If you've been in tick country, the best strategy is to visually check every half hour or so while hiking, do a thorough check before you get in the car, and then, when you take a posthike shower, do an even more thorough check of your entire body. Ticks that haven't latched on are easily removed but not easily killed. If I pick off a tick in the woods, I just toss it aside. If I find one on my person at home, I dispatch it and then send it down the toilet. For ticks that have embedded, removal with tweezers is best.

MOSQUITOES

Mosquitoes are common in the Carolinas, mountainous regions of both states excepted. Skeeters, along with no-see-ums, can plague coastal areas. Although it's very rare, individuals can become infected with the West Nile virus if bitten by an infected mosquito. Culex mosquitoes, the primary varieties that can transmit West Nile virus to humans, thrive in urban rather than natural areas. They lay their eggs in stagnant water and can breed in any standing water that remains for more than five days. Most people infected with West Nile virus have no symptoms of illness, but some may become ill, usually 3–15 days after being bitten.

Anytime you expect mosquitoes to be buzzing around, you may want to wear protective clothing, such as long sleeves, long pants, and socks. Loose-fitting, light-colored clothing is best. Spray clothing with insect repellent. Remember to follow the instructions on the repellent and to take extra care with children.

POISONOUS PLANTS

Recognizing poison ivy, oak, and sumac and avoiding contact with them are the most effective ways to prevent the painful, itchy rashes associated with these plants. In the Southeast, poison ivy ranges from a thick, tree-hugging vine to a shaded ground cover, 3 leaflets to a leaf; poison oak occurs as either a vine or shrub, with 3 leaflets as well; and poison sumac flourishes in swampland, each leaf containing 7–13 leaflets. Urushiol, the oil in the sap of these plants, is responsible for the rash. Usually within 12–14 hours of exposure (but sometimes much later), raised lines and/or blisters will appear, accompanied by a terrible itch. Refrain from scratching because bacteria under fingernails can cause infection. Wash and dry the rash thoroughly, applying a calamine lotion or other product to help dry out the rash. If itching or blistering is severe, seek medical attention. Remember that oil-contaminated clothes, pets, or hiking gear can easily cause an irritating rash on you or someone else, so wash not only any exposed parts of your body but also clothes, gear, and pets.

photographed by Tom Watson   *photographed by Jane Huber*   *photographed by Kevin Hansen/Freekee/Wikimedia Commons/CC0 (creativecommons.org /license/CC0)*

Poison Ivy   Poison Oak   Poison Sumac

CAMPGROUND ETIQUETTE

Here are a few tips on how to create good vibes with fellow campers and wildlife that you may encounter.

- **MAKE SURE YOU CHECK IN,** pay your fee, and mark your site as directed. Don't make the mistake of grabbing a seemingly empty site that looks more appealing than your site. It could be reserved. If you're unhappy with the site you've selected, check with the campground host for other options.

- **BE SENSITIVE TO THE GROUND BENEATH YOU.** Be sure to place all garbage in designated receptacles or pack it out if none is available. No one likes to see the trash someone else has left behind.

- **IT'S COMMON FOR ANIMALS TO WANDER THROUGH CAMPSITES,** where they may be accustomed to the presence of humans (and our food). An

One of the elk that roams Cataloochee Valley *(see campground 4, page 21)*

unannounced approach, a sudden movement, or a loud noise startles most animals. A surprised animal can be dangerous to you, to others, and to themselves. Give them plenty of space.

- **PLAN AHEAD.** Know your equipment, your ability, and the area where you are camping—and prepare accordingly. Be self-sufficient at all times; carry necessary supplies for changes in weather or other conditions. A well-executed trip is a satisfaction to you and to others.

- **BE COURTEOUS TO OTHER CAMPERS**, hikers, bikers, and anyone else you encounter.

- **STRICTLY FOLLOW THE CAMPGROUND'S RULES** regarding the building of fires. Never burn trash; the smoke smells horrible, and debris in a fire pit or grill is unsightly. Note that firewood must be certified and heat-treated.

HAPPY CAMPING

There is nothing worse than a bad camping trip, especially because it is so easy to have a great time. To assist with making your outing a happy one, here are some pointers.

- **RESERVE YOUR SITE IN ADVANCE**, especially if it's a weekend or a holiday, or if the campground is wildly popular. Many prime campgrounds require at least a six-month lead time on reservations. Check before you go.

- **PICK YOUR CAMPING BUDDIES WISELY.** A family trip is pretty straightforward, but you may want to reconsider including grumpy Uncle Fred, who doesn't like bugs, sunshine, or marshmallows. After you know who's going, make sure that everyone is on the same page regarding expectations of difficulty (amenities or the lack thereof, physical exertion, and so on), sleeping arrangements, and food requirements.

- **DON'T DUPLICATE EQUIPMENT,** such as cooking pots and lanterns, among campers in your party. Carry what you need to have a good time, but don't turn the trip into a cross-country moving experience.

- **DRESS FOR THE SEASON.** Educate yourself on the temperature highs and lows of the specific part of the state you plan to visit. It may be warm at night in the summer in your backyard, but up in the mountains it can be quite chilly.

- **PITCH YOUR TENT ON A LEVEL SURFACE,** preferably one covered with leaves, pine straw, or grass. Use a tarp or specially designed footprint to thwart ground moisture and to protect the tent floor. Do a little site maintenance, such as picking up the small rocks and sticks that can damage your tent floor and make sleep uncomfortable. If you have a separate tent rainfly but don't think you'll need it, keep it rolled up at the base of the tent in case it starts raining at midnight.

- **CONSIDER TAKING A SLEEPING PAD** if the ground makes you uncomfortable. Choose a pad that is full-length and thicker than you think you might need. This will not only keep your hips from aching on hard ground but will also help keep you warm. A wide range of thin, light, and inflatable pads is available at camping stores, and these are a much better choice than home air mattresses, which conduct heat away from the body and tend to deflate during the night.

- **IF YOU ARE NOT HIKING IN TO A PRIMITIVE CAMPSITE,** there is no real need to skimp on food due to weight. Plan tasty meals and bring everything you will need to prepare, cook, eat, and clean up.

- **IF YOU TEND TO USE THE BATHROOM MULTIPLE TIMES AT NIGHT,** you should plan ahead. Leaving a warm sleeping bag and stumbling around in the dark to find the restroom, whether it be a pit toilet, a fully plumbed comfort station, or just the woods, is not fun. Keep a flashlight and any other accoutrements you may need by the tent door and know exactly where to head in the dark.

- **STANDING DEAD TREES AND STORM-DAMAGED LIVING TREES** can pose a real hazard to tent campers. These trees may have loose or broken limbs that could fall at any time. When choosing a campsite or even just a spot to rest during a hike, look up.

VENTURING AWAY FROM THE CAMPGROUND

If you go for a hike, bike ride, or other excursion into the wilderness, here are some precautions to keep in mind.

- **ALWAYS CARRY FOOD AND WATER,** whether you are planning to go overnight or not. Food will give you energy, help keep you warm, and sustain you in an emergency until help arrives. Bring potable water or treat water by boiling or filtering before drinking from a lake or stream.

- **STAY ON DESIGNATED TRAILS.** Most hikers get lost when they leave the trail. Even on the most clearly marked trails, there is usually a point where you have to stop and consider which direction to head. If you become disoriented, don't panic. As soon as you think you may be off-track, stop, assess your current direction, and then retrace your steps back to the point where you went awry. If you have absolutely no idea how to continue, return to the trailhead the way you came in. Should you become completely lost and have no idea of how to return to the trailhead, remaining in place along the trail and waiting for help is most often the best option for adults and always the best option for children.

Mouse Creek Falls is just a 2-mile hike from Big Creek Campground *(see campground 2, page 15)*.

- **BE ESPECIALLY CAREFUL WHEN CROSSING STREAMS.** Whether you are fording the stream or crossing on a log, make every step count. If you have any doubt about maintaining your balance on a log, go ahead and ford the stream instead. When fording a stream, use a trekking pole or stout stick for balance and face upstream as you cross. If a stream seems too deep to ford, turn back. Whatever is on the other side is not worth risking your life.

- **BE CAREFUL AT OVERLOOKS.** Though these areas may provide spectacular views, they are potentially hazardous. Stay back from the edge of outcrops and be absolutely sure of your footing: a misstep can mean a nasty and possibly fatal fall.

- **KNOW THE SYMPTOMS OF HYPOTHERMIA.** Shivering and forgetfulness are the two most common indicators of this insidious killer. Hypothermia can occur at any elevation, even in the summer. Wearing cotton clothing puts you especially at risk because cotton, when wet, wicks heat away from the body. To prevent hypothermia, dress in layers of synthetic clothing for insulation, use a cap and gloves to reduce heat loss, and protect yourself with waterproof, breathable outerwear. If symptoms arise, get the victim to shelter, a fire, hot liquids, and dry clothes or a dry sleeping bag.

- **TAKE ALONG YOUR BRAIN.** A cool, calculating mind is the single most important piece of equipment you'll ever need on the trail. Think before you act. Watch your step. Plan ahead. Avoiding accidents before they happen is the best recipe for a rewarding and relaxing hike.

HELPFUL HINTS

To make the most of your tent-camping trip, explore the park's website. If going to a state or national park, download maps and other pertinent information before setting out. This way you can familiarize yourself with the area. Once there, ask questions. Most stewards of the land are proud of their terra firma and are happy to help you have the best time possible.

If traveling in the national forests of the Carolinas, order a forest map well before you leave home. Not only will a map make it that much easier to reach your destination, but nearby hikes, scenic drives, waterfalls, and landmarks will also be easier to find. Visit national forest visitor centers in addition to ranger stations. While there, seek any additional literature about the area in which you are interested.

In writing this book, I had the pleasure of meeting many friendly, helpful people: local residents proud of the unique lands around them, and state park and national forest employees who endured my endless questions. Even better were my fellow tent campers, who were eager to share their knowledge about their favorite spots. They already know what beauty lies on the horizon.

As the Carolinas become more populated, these lands become that much more precious. Enjoy them, protect them, and use them wisely.

NORTH CAROLINA MOUNTAINS

Chasteen Creek Cascade at Smokemont Campground (*see campground 15, page 54*)

Balsam Mountain Campground

Beauty ★★★★ Privacy ★★★ Spaciousness ★★ Quiet ★★★★ Security ★★★★ Cleanliness ★★★★

At 5,310 feet, Balsam Mountain is Great Smoky Mountains National Park's highest campground.

The rare spruce-fir forest that cloaks the highest elevations of the Smoky Mountains is among the primary reasons this mountain range was designated a national park. Covering 13,000 of the park's 500,000 acres, the forest composes the southern limit of this relic of the most recent ice age. More than 10,000 years ago, when glaciers covered much of the United States, woodlands much more reminiscent of those in Canada today migrated south. When the glaciers retreated, this forest survived on the highest points of the Smokies, creating an island of red spruce and Fraser fir trees.

So what does this have to do with tent camping? Well, it just so happens that Balsam Mountain Campground is located in a swath of this rare forest. Not only does it offer the highest tent camping within Great Smoky Mountains National Park, but it also offers campers a chance to experience this remarkable forest firsthand.

The campground was set up not long after the inception of the national park in 1934. Back then, few visitors drove or pulled oversize campers on the narrow, winding roads; the majority tent camped. So when the campground was set up, builders had tent campers in mind. Today, we can camp in the fine tradition of the first park visitors.

View of the Flat Creek chasm

KEY INFORMATION

CONTACT: Great Smoky Mountains National Park, 865-436-1200; nps.gov/grsm

OPEN: Mid-May–early October

SITES: 44

EACH SITE HAS: Picnic table, fire grate

WHEELCHAIR ACCESS: Yes

ASSIGNMENT: Reservations required (877-444-6777; recreation.gov)

REGISTRATION: Online or by phone before arrival

AMENITIES: Water spigot, flush toilet

PARKING: At campsites only

FEE: $17.50

ELEVATION: 5,310'

RESTRICTIONS:
PETS: On leash only

FIRES: In fire grates only

ALCOHOL: At campsites only

OTHER: 6 people/site; 14-day stay limit; 30' RV-length limit; food (and dishes and utensils) must be stored in vehicle when not in use; only certified heat-treated firewood allowed; quiet hours 10 p.m.–6 a.m.

Balsam Mountain sits on a rib ridge between the headwaters of Flat and Bunches Creeks. Past the entrance station, campsites are set along the main road.

You will immediately notice the sites' small size, a historical element of Balsam Mountain that discourages most of today's RV campers. But even with the small sites relatively close together, you will find ample privacy because the campground rarely fills to capacity.

Keeping south on the main road, come to a loop. Campsites are spread along this loop among the fir and spruce trees. The ground slopes off steeply away from the road, resulting in some unlevel sites. With a little scouting, however, you will find a good site among the evergreens.

Balsam Mountain is off the beaten national park path. In fact, the road leading to the campground connects to the Blue Ridge Parkway, which then connects to the main body of the park. There is only one trail in the area, but it is a winner: Flat Creek. Leave the Heintooga Picnic Area on this path, and enjoy a magnificent view of the main Smokies crest before descending to the perched watershed of Flat Creek. Cruise through an attractive high-elevation forest before reaching the side trail to Flat Creek Falls, a steep and narrow cascade. Backtrack or continue past the falls to cross Bunches Creek and reach Balsam Mountain Road.

Balsam Mountain Road, just one of many interesting forest drives in the immediate area, leads 8 miles to the Blue Ridge Parkway, the granddaddy of all scenic roads in the Southern Appalachian Mountains, with recreation opportunities to both the north and south. A more rustic forest drive leaves Heintooga Picnic Area on a gravel road and runs north along Balsam Mountain before descending into Straight Fork valley to emerge at the nearby Qualla Cherokee Indian Reservation. Several hiking trails are along the way, including Palmer Creek Trail—which descends into a beautiful, richly forested valley—and Hyatt Ridge Trail, which, along with Beech Gap Trail, makes for a rewarding high-country loop hike of 8 miles. Anglers can fish for trout on Straight Fork or enjoy many of the stream- and pond-fishing opportunities on the reservation. The nearby town of Cherokee has your typical Smokies tourist traps, as well as camping supplies.

Balsam Mountain Campground

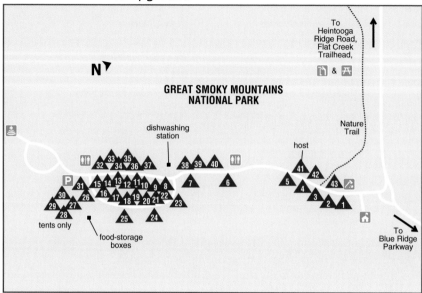

GETTING THERE

From the Oconaluftee Visitor Center near Cherokee, North Carolina, take Newfound Gap Road 0.5 mile south to the Blue Ridge Parkway. Turn left on the Blue Ridge Parkway, and follow it 10.8 miles to Heintooga Ridge Road. Turn left on Heintooga Ridge Road, and drive 8.4 miles to Balsam Mountain Campground, on your left.

GPS COORDINATES: N35° 33.902' W83° 10.465'

Big Creek Campground

Beauty ★★★★★ Privacy ★★★ Spaciousness ★★★★ Quiet ★★★★★ Security ★★★★ Cleanliness ★★★★

Only tents are allowed at this walk-in campground located in the Smokies' remote "Far East."

Great Smoky Mountains National Park has a reputation, somewhat undeserved, of being overcrowded. Sure, some places can become peopled, but if you know the right places to go, your time in the park can be a relaxing getaway. Big Creek Campground is one of those places. It is the Smokies' smallest campground and its sole tent-only campground. This walk-in campground is set deep in the woods adjacent to the pure mountain waters of Big Creek—so deep, in fact, that when you come to the campground parking area, you'll wonder where the campground is. (For your information, it's between the campground parking area and noisy Big Creek.)

A small footpath leaves the parking area and loops the 12 campsites in the shade of tall hardwoods. Since Big Creek is a walk-in campground, you must tote your camping supplies anywhere from 100 to 300 feet. But after that, you'll be hearing only the intonations of Big Creek and smelling the wildflowers rather than hearing RV engines and smelling exhaust fumes.

Five of the sites are directly creekside. Each is spacious enough for you to spread out your gear. The new tent pads are elevated and well drained. A somewhat-sparse understory reduces privacy, but the intimate walk-in setup magnifies an atmosphere of camaraderie among fellow campers not necessarily found in larger drive-in campgrounds.

Big Creek as seen from the trail bridge near Walnut Bottoms

KEY INFORMATION

CONTACT: Great Smoky Mountains National Park, 865-436-1200; nps.gov/grsm

OPEN: April–October

SITES: 12, 5 horse campsites

EACH SITE HAS: Picnic table, fire pit, lantern post

WHEELCHAIR ACCESS: No

ASSIGNMENT: Reservations required (877-444-6777; recreation.gov)

REGISTRATION: Online or by phone before arrival

AMENITIES: Cold water, flush toilets

PARKING: At campsites only

FEE: $17.50

ELEVATION: 1,700'

RESTRICTIONS:

PETS: On leash only

FIRES: In fire pits only

ALCOHOL: At campsites only

OTHER: 6 people/site; 14-day stay limit; no RVs or trailers; food (and dishes and utensils) must be stored in vehicle when not in use; only certified heat-treated firewood allowed; quiet hours 10 p.m.–6 a.m.

The campground comfort station borders the parking area. It houses flush toilets and a large sink with a cold-water faucet. Two other water spigots are found along the footpath loop. A recycling bin is located in the parking area.

You can explore the locale directly from your campsite. The Big Creek Trail starts at the campground and traces an old railroad grade from the logging era. Cool off the old-fashioned way in one of the many swimming holes that pool between the white rapids of Big Creek. Gaze up the sides of the valley; the rock bluffs you see have sheltered Smoky Mountain wayfarers for thousands of years. Hike 2 miles up Big Creek to find the tumbling cascades of Mouse Creek Falls. Falls often occur where a feeder creek enters a main stream; the primary stream valley erodes faster than the side stream valley, creating a hanging side canyon and then a waterfall. Continue on to Walnut Bottoms at 5 miles. Walnut Bottoms has historically had more man-bear encounters than anywhere in the park, so keep all food locked in your trunk, not in the seat of your car, when away from camp. Crestmont Lumber Company had a camp here in the early 1900s, but now the area has returned to its former splendor. If you wish to explore further, three other trails splinter from Walnut Bottoms.

How about a strenuous hike through old-growth forest to a mountaintop that's capped by a Canadian-type forest with a 360-degree view from a fire tower? It's 6 steep miles up the Baxter Creek Trail, but your efforts will be amply rewarded. Start at the Big Creek picnic area just below the

A trillium blooms in the Big Creek valley.

campground and go for it. Or take Mount Sterling Trail from Mount Sterling Gap on nearby NC 284. It's only 2.7 miles to the tower this way. Alternately, hike the Chestnut Branch Trail, leaving from the Big Creek Ranger Station. It leads 2 miles to the highest and wildest section of the entire Appalachian Trail in the South, traversing the Smoky Mountains. The historic fire tower at Mount Cammerer is only 4 miles farther. Or loop back on the Appalachian Trail to Davenport Gap, and road-walk a short piece back to the campground.

Big Creek is wilderness tent camping at its best. The walk-in setting is your first step into the natural world of the Smokies. The rest of your adventure is limited only by your desire to explore the 500,000 acres in Big Creek Campground's backyard.

Big Creek Campground

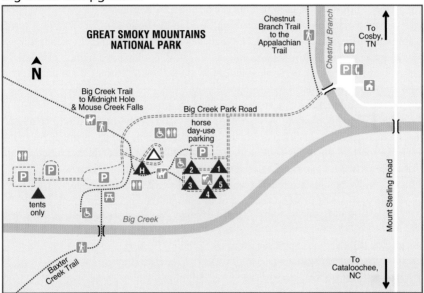

GETTING THERE

Take I-40 to Exit 451 for Waterville, North Carolina. Cross the Pigeon River, and immediately turn left then keep right on Waterville Road to follow the Pigeon upstream. Come to an intersection 2 miles after crossing the Pigeon. Proceed straight through the intersection onto Big Creek Entrance Road, and soon enter the park. Pass the Big Creek Ranger Station, and drive to the end of the gravel road and the campground after 1 mile.

GPS COORDINATES: N35° 45.093'   W83° 06.588'

Cable Cove Campground

Beauty ★★★★ Privacy ★★★ Spaciousness ★★★★★ Quiet ★★★★ Security ★★★★ Cleanliness ★★★★

Stay at Cable Cove and access the Smoky Mountains National Park by boat or land, free of traffic hassles.

This charming and sedate campground sits on former farmland once tilled by the Cable family. After World War II began, the demand for aluminum and the power to manufacture it soared, leading to the construction of nearby Fontana Dam, which began in 1942. Used to generate power to produce aluminum for the war, the dam remains an important source of energy. Prior to flooding behind the dam, the farming families moved away. The U.S. Forest Service moved in, later establishing a campground in the hollow.

Cable Cove's proximity to Fontana Lake makes it an ideal camp from which to visit the Smoky Mountains via boat, thus avoiding auto traffic. Fontana is a lightly used lake, with unlimited views of the park that are unspoiled by the troops of tourists that fill the highways on busy summer weekends.

Cable Cove Campground stretches out along a gravel road that slopes down toward Fontana Lake, 0.5 mile distant. A small loop at the end of the campground road enables drivers to turn around; this loop holds five campsites. Cable Creek, a small trout stream, parallels the road on the right. The campground is well maintained, quiet, and unassuming. Shortly after arriving, I felt as if I belonged there, like one of the neighbors.

The 10 creekside sites are heavily wooded and have a thick understory. They are spacious yet have an air of privacy because of the junglelike vegetation along Cable Creek. The 11 sites opposite the creek have a grassy, gladelike understory beneath second-growth

Kayaks ready to launch at the Cable Cove ramp

CONTACT: Cheoah Ranger District, Nantahala National Forest, 828-479-6431; www.fs.usda.gov/recarea/nfsnc /recarea/?recid=48634

OPEN: April–October

SITES: 26

EACH SITE HAS: Tent pad, picnic table, fire grate, lantern post

WHEELCHAIR ACCESS: Yes

ASSIGNMENT: First come, first served; no reservations

REGISTRATION: Self-registration

AMENITIES: Water, vault toilet

PARKING: At campsites only

FEE: $10

ELEVATION: 1,800'

RESTRICTIONS:

PETS: On leash only

FIRES: In fire grates only

ALCOHOL: At campsites only

OTHER: 14-day stay limit

trees that are reclaiming the old fields. During my stay, the grass had been freshly trimmed and looked especially attractive. This "yard" space makes for a more open camping area, one conducive to visiting your neighbor, a customary thing to do in friendly western North Carolina. These campsites are some of the largest I have ever seen, extending far back from the road. An area of brush and trees divides the upper and lower campgrounds. Beyond the brush are the five sites at the turnaround loop, in the deep woods adjacent to Cable Creek.

Three water spigots have been placed at even intervals in the linear campground. Two comfort stations with vault toilets are at either end of the campground; campers in the middle may have to walk a bit to use them. But even this stroll could be an opportunity to get to know your neighbor. I camped toward the middle, and by the time I left, the gravel road resembled a country lane—slow moving and full of good friends.

Most of your fellow campers will be boaters. A high-quality boat ramp is 0.5 mile away; campers use it to fish for bream, bass, trout, and walleye, as well as to access the national park. (Using a boat to access the park is a smart way to beat the crowds. I've been doing it for more than two decades and wonder why it hasn't caught on more.) Several hiking trails in the Smokies run right down to the lake. Check out the 360-degree view from Shuckstack Fire Tower. To reach the tower, which is visible from the lake, boat up the Eagle Creek arm of Fontana Lake. From the embayment, the Lost Cove Trail leads 3 miles up to the Appalachian Trail. Just 0.4 mile south on the Appalachian Trail is the tower. The outline of Fontana Lake is easily discerned from the tower. Look northeast and see the spine of the Smokies until it fades from view.

Across the water from Cable Cove is famed Hazel Creek, whose trout waters have been featured in fishing websites and magazines for years. But don't visit just for the fish. Hike up the gentle trail that parallels the creek to discover relics of the Smokies' past, including old homesites, fields, and mining endeavors. Wide bridges spanning the creek make this walk even more pleasant. You can only access this part of the Smokies by boat or a very long walk; if you don't have a boat, contact Fontana Marina at 828-498-2129 to arrange for a shuttle. The marina is only 4 miles west of Cable Cove. You can purchase limited supplies at the small store at Fontana Village Resort near the marina, but you're better off stocking up in Maryville,

Tennessee, if you are coming from the Volunteer State, or in Robbinsville, North Carolina, south of Cable Cove on NC 143.

Also near Fontana Marina stands the engineering marvel that is Fontana Dam, the tallest dam east of the Rockies at 480 feet, and well worth a visit. A visitor center recounts the story of the dam, and cable cars take visitors down to its powerhouse. You can cross the dam in your auto—the landlubber's way to access the Smokies—at one of the more remote trailheads. From this trailhead, trace the Appalachian Trail 3.3 miles up to Shuckstack and its tower. Or take the undulating Lakeshore Trail through the Smokies' lush flora 5 miles to Eagle Creek and its embayment. Whether you get there by land or water, this slice of the Smokies is a gem to visit.

Cable Cove Campground

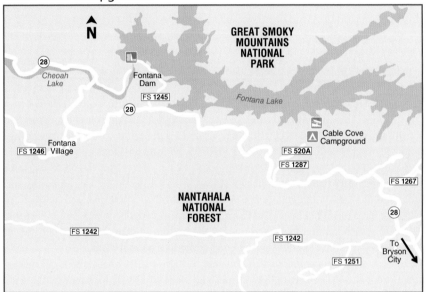

GETTING THERE

From Fontana Village, North Carolina, take NC 28 east 4.7 miles. Turn left on FS 1287/FS 520A/Cable Cove Road, and go 1 mile. Cable Cove will be on your right.

GPS COORDINATES: N35° 25.890' W83° 45.216'

⛺ Cataloochee Campground

Beauty ★★★★★ Privacy ★★★★ Spaciousness ★★★★★ Quiet ★★★★★ Security ★★★★ Cleanliness ★★★★

Cataloochee Valley's remoteness and inaccessibility make it one of the Smokies' better-kept secrets.

Cataloochee Campground is only the first attractive spot you'll see in this valley of meadows, streams, mountains, history—and elk, which have been introduced into the valley and offer extraordinary wildlife viewing in Cataloochee's meadows. The celebrated fishing waters of Cataloochee Creek form one border of the campground, while a small feeder stream forms the other. In between is a flat, attractive camping area canopied with stately white pines. The attractions of Cataloochee Valley have increased the remote valley's popularity, resulting in reservations being required for all campers at Cataloochee Campground.

Cataloochee Valley has ideal summer weather, with warm days and cool nights. The 2,600-foot elevation is fairly high for a valley campground with a stream the size of Cataloochee

Admiring one of the big poplars

KEY INFORMATION

CONTACT: Great Smoky Mountains National Park, 865-436-1200; nps.gov/grsm

OPEN: Late March–October

SITES: 27

EACH SITE HAS: Picnic table, fire pit, lantern post

WHEELCHAIR ACCESS: Yes

ASSIGNMENT: Reservations required (877-444-6777; recreation.gov)

REGISTRATION: Online before arrival

AMENITIES: Cold water, flush toilets

PARKING: At campsites only

FEE: $25

ELEVATION: 2,610'

RESTRICTIONS:

PETS: On leash only

FIRES: In fire pits only

ALCOHOL: At campsites only

OTHER: 6 people/site; 14-day stay limit; 31' trailer-length limit (though not recommended for trailers over 25'); food (and dishes and utensils) must be stored in vehicle when not in use; only certified heat-treated firewood allowed; quiet hours 10 p.m.–6 a.m.

Creek. Cataloochee uses the basic campground design: campsites splintering off a loop road. Six sites lie along Cataloochee Creek; a few others border the small feeder stream. All are roomy and placed where the pines allow. An erratic understory of hemlock and rhododendron leaves privacy to the luck of which site you draw. The campground host is situated at the entrance for your safety and convenience. Be forewarned: bears are sighted yearly at this campground, so properly store your food and keep the wild in the Smoky Mountain bears.

Most RV campers shy away from this campground because the National Park Service advises against RVs making the long drive over rough, gravel roads. Cataloochee fills up on summer weekends, yet, with only 27 sites, it doesn't seem overly crowded. A comfort station is next to the campground at the head of the host. It has flush toilets and a cold-water faucet that pours into a large sink. Another water spigot is at the other end of the campground.

With all there is to do, you'll probably stay here only to rest from perusing the park. The first order of business is an auto tour of Cataloochee Valley. To gain a feel for the area, get a copy of the handy park-service pamphlet at the ranger station. An old church, a school, and numerous homesites are a delight to explore. Informative displays further explain about life long ago in this part of the world.

Cataloochee Valley is a hiker's paradise. Take the Boogerman Trail 7.4 undulating miles through different vegetation zones. The trail, which begins and ends at Caldwell Fork Trail, loops among old-growth hemlocks and tulip trees. Old homesites add a touch of human history; numerous footbridges make exploring this watery mountain land fun and easy on the feet. Or take the Little Cataloochee Trail to Little Cataloochee Church. Set in the backwoods, the church was built in 1890 and is still used today. Other signs of humanity that you'll see include a ramshackle cabin, chimneys, fence posts, and rock walls.

The Cataloochee Divide Trail starts at 4,000 feet and rambles along the ridgeline border that straddles the Maggie and Cataloochee Valleys. To the north is the rugged green expanse of the national park, and to the south are the developed areas along US 19. Grassy knolls along the way make good viewing and relaxing spots.

Using the Rough Fork, Caldwell Fork, and Fork Ridge Trails, you can make another loop, this one 9.3 miles. Pass the fields of the Woody Place; then climb Fork Ridge, descend to

Caldwell Fork, and climb Fork Ridge yet again to experience the literal highs and lows of Appalachian hiking.

The meadows of Cataloochee Valley are an ideal setting for a picnic. Decide on your favorite view and lay down your blanket. Nearby shady streams will serenade you as you look up at the wooded ridges that line the valley. Elk, deer, and other critters feed at the edges of the fields, drawing in nature photographers. Dusk is an ideal time to see Cataloochee's wildlife.

During my last stay at this campground, summer weather had finally hit. The air had a lazy, hazy feel as I toured the valley's historic structures. I fished away the afternoon, catching and releasing a few rainbows downstream from the campground. After grilling hamburgers for supper, I walked up Rough Fork Trail to the Woody Place. The homestead looked picturesque as the late-evening sunlight filtered through the nearby forest. As I came back to the trailhead, deer browsed in the Cataloochee meadow. I knew I had come to the right place. So will you.

Cataloochee Campground

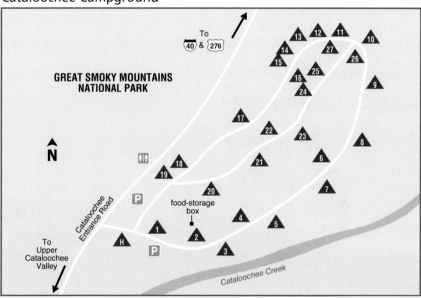

GETTING THERE

In North Carolina, take I-40 to Exit 20; then drive south on US 276. Follow it a short distance, then immediately turn right on Cove Creek Road, which you follow 5.7 miles to enter the park. Beyond the park boundary, in 1.8 miles turn left onto the paved Cataloochee Entrance Road, and follow it 3.1 miles. The campground will be on your left.

GPS COORDINATES: N35° 37.881'   W83° 05.191'

Doughton Park Campground

Beauty ★★★★ Privacy ★★★ Spaciousness ★★★ Quiet ★★★ Security ★★★★ Cleanliness ★★★★★

Doughton Park Campground is much more than a way station along the Blue Ridge Parkway.

The National Park Service does a really good job with this Blue Ridge Parkway campground, which is located on the crest of the Blue Ridge. A smart design spreads the campsites out among several loops and makes the area seem like several small campgrounds. The tent and RV sites are divided into separate sections, which makes it even better. Twenty-one of the campsites can be reserved.

The 6,430-acre park and campground are named after former North Carolina Representative "Muley Bob" Doughton, who fought hard to help the parkway become the scenic reality it is. He would be proud of this area, which unobtrusively integrates modern structures into the historic dwellings and hiking trails that lace the park.

Before you explore Doughton Park, pick a campsite. This may take a few minutes, as the campground has several distinct areas. Open and airy, it is tastefully landscaped and well integrated into the ridgetop setting. Even the most discriminating tent campers will find a site to suit their tastes.

Doughton Park evokes a mountain ambience.

photographed by T. W. Buckner/Flickr

KEY INFORMATION

CONTACT: Blue Ridge Parkway, 828-298-0398; nps.gov/blri

OPEN: Late May–late October

SITES: 109, 24 RV sites

EACH SITE HAS: Tent pad, picnic table, fire ring

WHEELCHAIR ACCESS: Yes

ASSIGNMENT: First come, first served and by reservation (877-444-6777; recreation.gov)

REGISTRATION: At campground hut

AMENITIES: Water, flush toilets

PARKING: At campsites only; 2 vehicles/site

FEE: $20

ELEVATION: 3,600'

RESTRICTIONS:

PETS: On 6' or shorter leash

FIRES: In fire rings only

ALCOHOL: At campsites only

OTHER: 6 people/site; 30-day total stay limit in calendar year across all Blue Ridge Parkway campgrounds; food (and dishes and utensils) must be stored in vehicle when not in use; only certified heat-treated firewood allowed; quiet hours 10 p.m.–6 a.m.

B or C Loops are the place for tent campers, as the A Loop is reserved for RV campers. The first part of B Loop holds 22 sites and is heavily wooded, yet with a light understory. The sites undulate along a hill and are fairly close, so you may be a tad cozy with your neighbor. The comfort station is a ways down a sloping path, possibly a little farther than some are willing to walk.

Continuing along B Loop, sites 23–33 are set back in the woods, down from the paved campground road. Short paths lead back to them, so you will have to carry your gear to your site. This distance allows for the most rustic camping experience, out of sight from vehicles. The sites closest to the parking area border a grassy field adjacent to the parking area. Campers share the comfort station with the first loop via a short, paved path.

The rest of B Loop circles the highest point of the campground. It has 30 sites and is centered on a grassy glade where a water tank sits. Oddly enough, a campsite is located right by the water tank; when I checked it out, I found the view of the surrounding mountain lands worth the intrusion of the green structure. Other sites here offer intermittent views of the Blue Ridge and beyond. You even have a view from the comfort station at the loop's center.

The C Loop (which has been closed in the past but was open at press time) continues along the ridge and passes a few sites for larger pop-up tent campers, then enters a loop featuring a campfire circle. Here, 11 sites are situated in an attractive meadow. Trees have been strategically planted by each campsite for shade and aesthetic appeal.

Beyond the campfire circle, the C Loop winds amid hilly forestland, rolling and dipping among rock outcrops. Another 20 sites are situated where the land allows. Because the loop is at the very back of the campground, you will encounter few vehicles. A comfort station is centered on this loop as well.

The Blue Ridge Parkway is an exercise in scenic beauty, but I think this particular area is exceptional even for the BRP. A drive in either direction will sate your taste for dramatic landscapes and historic sites. The Brinegar Cabin is just a short distance north. Of course, the most rewarding views are those earned with a little sweat.

Doughton Park has more than 30 miles of trails that meander through pastures, along wooded ridges, and by mountain streams. The Bluff Mountain Trail departs from the campground and gives you a sampling of this country. It extends for 3 or so miles in each direction. The Fodderstack Trail, a 2-mile round trip, climbs to the Wildcat Rocks Overlook. Another recommended trail is Basin Creek, which ends at the Caudill Cabin (only accessible by foot). Cedar Ridge Trail begins at the Brinegar Cabin and drops down to Basin Creek. Before you hike any of these trails, download a Doughton Park trail map from the Blue Ridge Parkway website. Then get out there and stretch your legs after enjoying that fantastic Blue Ridge Parkway scenery.

Doughton Park Campground

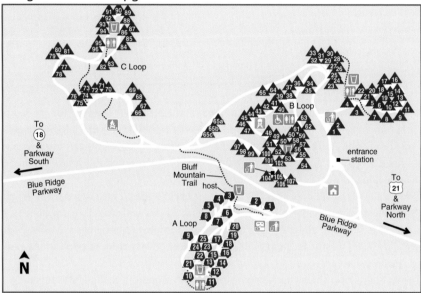

GETTING THERE

From the intersection of US 21 and NC 18 in Sparta, North Carolina, take NC 18 southwest 14.4 miles to the Blue Ridge Parkway. Turn north on the parkway, and drive 8.7 miles to milepost 239. Doughton Park Campground will be on your left.

GPS COORDINATES: N36° 25.717'   W81° 09.369'

6

Julian Price Park Campground

Beauty ★★★★★ Privacy ★★★ Spaciousness ★★★★ Quiet ★★★★ Security ★★★★ Cleanliness ★★★★★

This campground is part of the Blue Ridge Parkway, yet it offers more than just a stopping place between scenic drives.

High in the forests of the Blue Ridge Mountains, Julian Price Memorial Park offers good camping and plenty of activities that don't involve an automobile. Don't let the size of the campground scare you off. There are nearly 200 sites in three areas: one area for RV camping only, one for one-night camping only, and another for both RV and tent camping.

The one-night-only camping loop backs against the shores of Price Lake. The south end of the paved loop is thickly forested, both overhead and on the ground, for maximum privacy. Five sites are right along the lakeshore. The other end of the loop circles a field and is more open. A few pull-through RV sites are here. A lighted bathroom is conveniently placed at the center of the loop for all campers to share. Two water spigots are located at each end of this spacious, private loop.

The main RV and tent area has three loops. Loops C and D spur off the larger Loop B. Oddly enough, Loop D is actually inside Loop B; Loop C spurs off on its own. All are in a

A spring afternoon on the Blue Ridge Parkway

KEY INFORMATION

CONTACT: Blue Ridge Parkway, 828-298-0398; nps.gov/blri

OPEN: Mid-May–late-October

SITES: 121, 75 RV sites

EACH SITE HAS: Tent pad, picnic table, fire grate, lantern post

WHEELCHAIR ACCESS: Yes

ASSIGNMENT: First come, first served and by reservation (877-444-6777; recreation.gov)

REGISTRATION: Register at campground check-in station

AMENITIES: Water, flush toilets

PARKING: At campsites only; 2 vehicles/site

FEE: $20

ELEVATION: 3,400'

RESTRICTIONS:

PETS: On 6' or shorter leash

FIRES: In fire grates only

ALCOHOL: At campsites only

OTHER: 6 people/site; 30-day total stay limit in calendar year across all Blue Ridge Parkway campgrounds; 30' trailer-length limit; food (and dishes and utensils) must be stored in vehicle when not in use; only certified heat-treated firewood allowed; quiet hours 10 p.m.–6 a.m.

rolling woodland and are set into the mountains without dominating the natural landscape. The plethora of trees overhead reminds you that you are in the forest. The rhododendron understory provides plenty of privacy; however, it isn't everywhere, which means you can move about the campground freely. Landscaping timbers were used where site leveling was necessary. Some of the sites in Loops B and C are a tad close together, but with investigating and luck, you can find a private site. Prepare to search for the site you find desirable. Nine water spigots are scattered throughout these three loops for easy water access, and three lighted bathrooms ensure that you never have to go too far if nature calls in the middle of the night.

Loops E and F are for RVs only and concentrate these campers in one location. On my visit to Price Park, I didn't see any other RVers outside of E or F, with the exception of a couple in the one-night-only loop. Expect a full house on hot summer weekends, when nearby lowlanders escape the heat. However, I would take my chances on a first visit to find a site you prefer in person, then note your favorite sites to make reservations on future visits. A ranger and a campground host reside at the campground to answer questions and ease your safety concerns.

Even the most ardent auto tourists have to stretch their legs every once in a while and see for themselves just what is beyond the roadside. Price Park offers the Blue Ridge sightseer plenty to do outside the car. Trails run through the campground, which makes starting a hike even easier.

The Boone Fork Trail makes a 5-mile loop passing through many environments of the Blue Ridge. It leaves the campground to enter a meadow and picks up an old farm road. It then runs along Bee Tree Creek, crossing it 16 times. Pass through a rocky area and return to the campground through a meadow.

The 2.3-mile Green Knob Trail climbs to an overlook that will reward you with well-earned views of Price Lake, then loops back via Sims Pond. The Tanawha Trail runs 13 miles south along the Blue Ridge Parkway and obviously requires a shuttle. A segment of the nearly complete North Carolina Mountains-to-Sea Trail passes through Price Park on its way to the Atlantic.

The Price Lake Trail makes a 2.3-mile loop around the 47-acre scenic tarn, which contains three species of trout that you can angle for: rainbow, brook, and brown. Nearby Sims Pond has only the native brook trout. Stream anglers can try Boone Fork and Sims Creek for trout as well. A valid North Carolina fishing license is required. Additionally, canoes and kayaks can be rented to paddle Price Lake.

During the 1940s, Julian Price bought this area as a retreat for his company employees. His heirs willed the area to the National Park Service for all of us to enjoy. As scenic as the Blue Ridge Parkway is, you may find this special area hard to pass. Stop and spend a day enjoying the sights without a windshield between you and nature.

Julian Price Park Campground

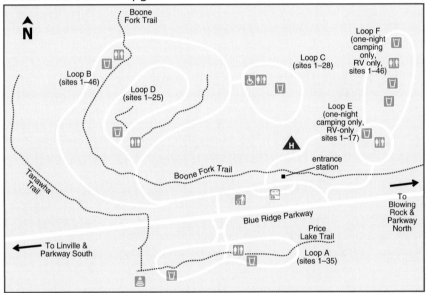

GETTING THERE

From Boone, North Carolina, take US 321 S for 6.3 miles to the Blue Ridge Parkway. Turn south on the parkway, and follow it 5 miles to Julian Price Memorial Park. The campground check-in station will be on your right.

GPS COORDINATES: N36° 08.365'   W81° 44.307'

7

Lake James State Park Campgrounds

Beauty ★★★★★ Privacy ★★★ Spaciousness ★★★ Quiet ★★★ Security ★★★★★ Cleanliness ★★★★★

All the sites here are walk-ins, and most are directly on Lake James.

Lake James, fed by the fine waters of the Pisgah River, is one of the cleanest, clearest lakes in the Carolinas. It also has some of the best views, as the high mountains of the Pisgah National Forest burst skyward beyond the water to the northwest. Lake James State Park features three camping options: the 20 walk-in sites at the Catawba River Area, the Paddy's Creek Area with 33 drive-in sites, and finally the 30 boat-in-only sites on Long Arm Peninsula.

The Catawba River Area campground is ideal for tent campers. Its nice bathhouse and two wheelchair-access campsites, 19 and 20, are immediately adjacent to the walk-in parking area. A foot trail leads toward Lake James and the other campsites. Tulip trees and other hardwoods shade the peninsula jutting into the deeply colored water. Reach campsites 1, 2, and 3 on the perimeter of a small knob where the campground woodyard stands. Pine and locust trees shade these sites, two of which are cut into a hill.

Another trail circles down to the lake and the lakeside campsites. Site 4 is on a scenic point overlooking the lake. Shortoff and Table Rock Mountains are easily visible in the distance. A wood fence borders the site along the lake, as it is a good 20 feet off a bluff down to the water. Site 5 is long and narrow. Site 6, shaded by pines, overlooks the lake. Site 7 is on the small side. Site 8 is highly coveted for its views. Cut into the mountainside, site 9 sits 30 feet back from the lake. Site 10 has numerous landscaping timbers that tier down to the lake, where a tiny beach overlooks a cove. Site 11 sits back from the water a bit, while site 12 is directly on the cove. Smallish site 13 is shaded by white pines. The water laps up to site 15. Site 16 is in a small flat. Site 17 is near an old foundation with steps leading to the lake. Site 18 is ideal for solitude seekers, set back in the woods by itself with a path leading only to it.

Water spigots are adequately spaced throughout, and trails lead back to the bathhouse. The Catawba River Area campground fills on good-weather weekends from late spring until Labor Day, but sites are available through the week anytime the campground is open.

A dock at Lake James State Park on a spring day

KEY INFORMATION

CONTACT: 828-652-5047; ncparks.gov /lake-james-state-park

OPEN: Year-round

SITES: Catawba River Area: 20; Paddy's Creek Area: 33; Long Arm Peninsula: 30

EACH SITE HAS: Tent pad, picnic table, fire ring, lantern post, bear-proof food-storage locker

WHEELCHAIR ACCESS: Yes

ASSIGNMENT: First come, first served and by reservation (877-722-6762; ncparks.gov /make-reservation); reservations required for Long Arm Peninsula

REGISTRATION: Ranger will come by to register you

AMENITIES: Hot showers, water spigots, flush toilets (Long Arm Peninsula: toilets only)

PARKING: Catawba River Area: at parking area for walk-in sites; Paddy's Creek Area: at campsites only, 2 vehicles/site

FEE: $10–$23

ELEVATION: 1,240'

RESTRICTIONS:

PETS: On leash only

FIRES: In fire rings only

ALCOHOL: Prohibited

OTHER: 6 people/site; 14-day stay limit; gates closed 7–10 p.m. (depending on season) to 7 a.m.

The Paddy's Creek Area sites are more open but well constructed. Some sites are terraced. The sites stretch along two roads, centered by a bathhouse. Each site has two parking spaces and plenty of room for your tent, so if you don't feel like carrying your stuff to the walk-in sites of the Catawba River Area, stay here.

Many campers use Lake James State Park as a base camp to explore western North Carolina, from Linville Gorge and the Blue Ridge Parkway to Asheville and the Biltmore Estate. Other campers remain within the confines of the park.

Lake James comprises 6,510 acres of alluring water and has 150 miles of shoreline, 5 miles of which are within the park. The swim beach is popular with campers during the summer (expect the water to be a tad cooler than that of your average lake). Canoes and kayaks are available for rent during the summer.

Those with boats will be launching at one of two nearby ramps to explore the water and shoreline. Cool, deep Lake James harbors largemouth and smallmouth bass, bream, and walleye. The park includes 13.2 miles of mountain biking trails and 12.6 miles of hiking trails. When you add up the aquatic and land opportunities with the fine tent camping here, Lake James State Park is worth a visit—and maybe several when you see it in person.

GETTING THERE

From I-40 in North Carolina, take Exit 90, head north on Fairview Road, and go 0.4 mile. Turn right on Harmony Grove Road, and go 2.1 miles. Turn left on US 70 W, and go 0.2 mile. Turn right on NC 126 E, and go 2.7 miles to the Catawba River Area on your left. Go another 4.6 miles, turn right on Rock Hill Street, and go 2.1 miles to reach the Paddy's Creek Area.

GPS COORDINATES:
   CATAWBA RIVER AREA: N35° 43.938'   W81° 53.997'
   PADDY'S CREEK AREA: N35° 45.414'   W81° 52.501'

Lake James State Park Overview

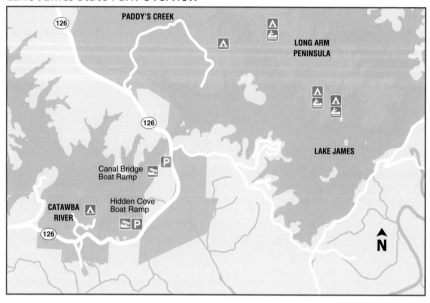

Lake James State Park Campgrounds

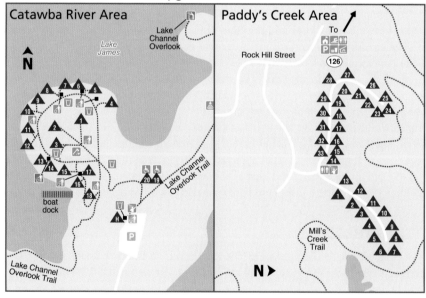

8

Lake Powhatan Campground

Beauty ★★★★ Privacy ★★★★ Spaciousness ★★★★ Quiet ★★★★ Security ★★★★★ Cleanliness ★★★★★

This attractive, well-maintained mountain biker's heaven is on Asheville's doorstep.

Lake Powhatan is a nicely developed, well-maintained recreation destination. While it is a great destination in its own right, Lake Powhatan's proximity to Asheville adds the possibilities of visiting tourist destinations in the area, such as the grand Biltmore Estate. Hikers, mountain bikers, and lake enthusiasts will also find much to do at this Pisgah National Forest destination.

The groomed campground is divided into four loops situated on wooded hills above the lake. The Big John Loop has 21 sites—mostly shaded by a pine, oak, and hickory forest—and it is the highest of them all. Each site has been leveled with landscaping timbers, despite the hilliness. Large and attractive, the sites here provide ample privacy. The Bent Creek Loop has sites 22–35. It also has hilly, large camps with rich woods. All the sites here are in great condition. The Lakeside Loop, with sites 36–57, is actually well above Lake Powhatan, though a few of the sites overlook the water. The sites here are the shadiest, sheltered by hemlock trees.

The Hardtime Loop, with sites 58–97, is my favorite. It's older than the others and looks a little more worn, yet it's well kept. This least-used loop, set on a ridgeline rife with dogwoods, actually has two loops. There are many attractive sites to choose from; you just have to be a little pickier. You will enjoy the pretty forest up here.

The Powhatan Mountains frame Lake Powhatan.

photographed by Jennifer Pharr Davis

KEY INFORMATION

CONTACT: Pisgah Ranger District, Pisgah National Forest, 828-670-5627; www.fs.usda.gov/recarea/nfsnc /recarea/?recid=48114

OPEN: March–October (Lakeside and Big John Loops: March–December)

SITES: 95

EACH SITE HAS: Picnic table, fire ring, lantern post; most have tent pads. Lakeside Loop: electric, water, sewer

WHEELCHAIR ACCESS: Yes

ASSIGNMENT: First come, first served and by reservation (877-444-6777; recreation.gov)

REGISTRATION: At entrance station

AMENITIES: Hot showers, water, flush toilets

PARKING: At campsites only; 2 vehicles/site

FEE: $22; $28 electric

ELEVATION: 2,100'

RESTRICTIONS:

PETS: On leash only

FIRES: In fire rings only

ALCOHOL: At campsites only

OTHER: Reservations must be made 4 days ahead of arrival and can be made up to 6 months in advance. No boats allowed on lake. Gate closed 10 p.m.–7 a.m.

The campground is gated and manned with hosts who help keep the place in good, clean shape. Water spigots are conveniently set throughout. All the loops except Bent Creek have showers, but Bent Creek does have a restroom. Lake Powhatan can and does fill on summer holidays, but the reservation system will assure you of a campsite whenever you desire. Take advantage of it.

Bent Creek was dammed to form Lake Powhatan, an impoundment that is attractive to both swimmers and anglers. One side of the lake has a large beach and swimming area, while the other side has a fishing pier. The lake is stocked with rainbow, brook, and brown trout, and you can also fish Bent Creek. No boats are allowed on the lake.

A network of hiking and mountain-biking trails weaves out from Lake Powhatan. The whole area is within the confines of the Bent Creek Research and Demonstration Forest. On the way in you will pass several national forest mountain-biking trailheads. Here you can make loops aplenty in the greater Bent Creek watershed, including up Wolf Creek, Ledford Branch, and Boyd Branch. Milder nature trails head directly out of the campground; one track circles the lake. Deerfield Loop and Pine Tree Trail let you explore the woods without getting in your car. The former winds through a variety of ecosystems surrounding Lake Powhatan; the latter has interpretive information that helps you understand the forest through which you walk. Homestead Loop is a short trail that passes over Lake Powhatan Dam. You do have to get in your car, but it is a short distance to visit the North Carolina Arboretum, which you will pass on your way in. Stop at the visitor center to learn more about this outdoor learning center.

Asheville is just a few miles up I-26, and you'll find all manner of activities there.

The national forest offers interpretive programs between Memorial Day and Labor Day. Many of these are tailored to kids of all ages, so you can keep junior busy while you get that much-needed R & R time.

Lake Powhatan Campground

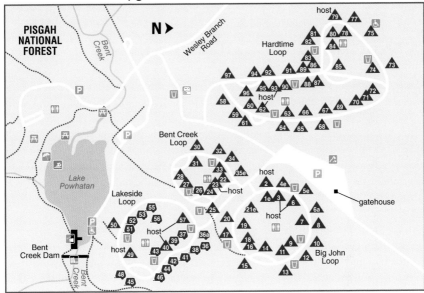

GETTING THERE

From Exit 33 on I-26 in Asheville, North Carolina, take NC 191 S for 2 miles to the signed right turn onto Bent Creek Ranch Road at a traffic light. In 0.3 mile keep straight (slight left) to take Wesley Branch Road 2.5 miles to the campground. The campground's address is 375 Wesley Branch Road, Asheville, NC 28806.

GPS COORDINATES: N35° 29.010'   W82° 37.512'

9

Linville Falls Campground

Beauty ★★★ Privacy ★★★ Spaciousness ★★★★ Quiet ★★★ Security ★★★★★ Cleanliness ★★★★★

Linville Falls lies at the head of the rugged Linville Gorge Wilderness.

The Blue Ridge Parkway is an unusual national park. It is linear, stretching 469 miles on the spine of the Southern Appalachians, connecting the Great Smoky Mountains and Shenandoah National Parks. When deciding to designate the first national park in our Southern mountains, government officials just couldn't decide between Shenandoah and the Smokies, so both were developed. Because of this compromise, the scenic road connecting them was built. In the process, officials brought many historic sites and attractive natural features under the park-service umbrella. One of these outstanding areas is Linville Falls, the crown jewel of Linville Gorge, which many consider the most scenic wilderness in the Tar Heel State.

Linville Falls Campground, just off the parkway, can be your base for exploring the gorge. This campground is fairly large, with 70 sites, 50 of which are for tent campers. Oddly, the tent and trailer sites are intermixed along two paved camping loops with paved pull-ins. The setting, at 3,200 feet in elevation, is a flat alongside the clean, clear Linville River. A mixture of white pine, hardwoods, rhododendron, and open grassy areas allows

Linville Falls, as seen from the end of the Plunge Basin Trail

KEY INFORMATION

CONTACT: Blue Ridge Parkway, 704-298-0398; nps.gov/blri

OPEN: Mid-May–October

SITES: 44, 18 RV sites

EACH SITE HAS: Picnic table, fire grate, grill

WHEELCHAIR ACCESS: Yes

ASSIGNMENT: First come, first served and by reservation (877-444-6777; recreation.gov)

REGISTRATION: At campground entrance booth

AMENITIES: Water spigot, flush toilets

PARKING: At campsites only; 2 vehicles/site

FEE: $20

ELEVATION: 3,200'

RESTRICTIONS:

PETS: On 6' or shorter leash

FIRES: In fire grates only

ALCOHOL: At campsites only

OTHER: 6 people/site; 30-day total stay limit in calendar year across all Blue Ridge Parkway campgrounds; 30' trailer-length limit; food (and dishes and utensils) must be stored in vehicle when not in use; only certified heat-treated firewood allowed; quiet hours 10 p.m.–6 a.m.

campers to choose the amount of sun and shade they want. Along Loop A are several appealing tent sites set in the woods directly riverside.

On Loop B two groupings of tent sites lie beneath beech trees. Your best bet is to cruise the loops and look for the site that most appeals to you. A sizable grassy meadow is free of campsites and makes for a great sunning or relaxing spot. The biggest drawback to the campground is its mixed placement of tent and trailer campsites. Nonetheless, choosy tent campers will be able to find a good spot. Water spigots are scattered about the campground, and the two bathroom facilities are located within easy walking distance of all the sites. For your safety and convenience, campground hosts and park personnel are on-site in the warm season. During winter, the water is turned off and vault toilets are used.

Linville Falls is your mandatory first destination. The falls, in two sections, drop at the point where the Linville River descends into its famous gorge. A park visitor center near the campground is your departure point. The Erwins View Trail is a 1.6-mile round-trip that takes hikers by four overlooks, passing the upper and lower falls. The Upper Falls View comes first. You can see both falls from Chimney View. The Gorge View allows a look down into the deep swath cut by the Linville River as it descends between Linville Mountain and Jonas Ridge. Erwins View offers an even more expansive vista than the previous three. Another hike leads steeply from the visitor center down to the Plunge Basin, at the base of the falls. To access the main gorge, managed under the auspices of the U.S. Forest Service, campers must drive a short distance to Wisemans View Road and the Kistler Memorial Highway, a scenic auto destination rivaling the Blue Ridge Parkway. Below, the Linville Gorge Wilderness covers nearly 11,000 acres. Wisemans View is particularly scenic, allowing visitors to gaze up the gorge. Hikers have to trace steep and very challenging trails to reach the river down in the gorge, and I know firsthand that they're pretty tough once you are in the gorge. A trail map of the gorge is available at the parkway visitor center. Bynum Bluff Trail makes a sharp drop down to a sharp bend in the river. Babel Tower Trail ends at a rocky prominence encircled by the Linville River on three sides. Before taking off on any of these trails, you might want to get a hearty meal in the nearby Linville Falls community, where you can also buy limited camping supplies.

Linville Falls Campground

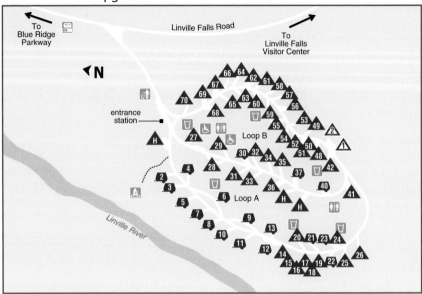

GETTING THERE

From the intersection of US 19E and NC 226 in Spruce Pine, North Carolina, drive south on NC 226 for 4.6 miles to the Blue Ridge Parkway. Head north on the parkway 14.5 miles to milepost 316.3 and Linville Falls. Turn right on Linville Falls Road, and go 0.5 mile to the campground.

GPS COORDINATES: N35° 58.110'   W81° 55.899'

10

Mount Mitchell State Park Campground

Beauty ★★★★★ Privacy ★★★★ Spaciousness ★★★ Quiet ★★★★ Security ★★★★★ Cleanliness ★★★★★

Mount Mitchell is the highest point in the eastern United States and has the highest tent-only campground.

Bring warm clothes with you to Mount Mitchell. The rarefied air up here calls to mind Canada more than Dixie. The flora and fauna follow suit. In 1915 then-Governor Locke Craig recognized the special character of this mountaintop and made it North Carolina's first state park. Now, with a tent-only campground and some superlative highland scenery, Mount Mitchell State Park is a Southern Appalachian highlight.

As the most recent ice age retreated north, cold-weather plants and animals retreated with them—except for those that survived on the highest peaks down in Dixie. These mountaintops formed, in effect, cool-climate islands where the northern species continue to survive. Mount Mitchell's campground is for tents only, unless you can carry an RV from the parking area up the stone steps to the campground. The short walk immediately enters the dense forest once dominated by the Fraser fir. Today, stunted and weather-beaten mountain ash and a few other hardwoods mingle with the firs.

The nine campsites splinter off the gravel path that rises with the mountainside. Set into the land amid the dense woods, they are small and fairly close together but private due to the heavy plant growth. There is little canopy overhead, as the trees become gnarled the higher they grow. Two water spigots lie along the short path; a bathroom with flush toilets is midway along the path. Firewood is sold by the bundle in the parking area.

A picnic shelter in Mount Mitchell State Park, with Mount Craig in the background

KEY INFORMATION

CONTACT: 828-675-4611; ncparks.gov
/mount-mitchell-state-park

OPEN: May–October

SITES: 9

EACH SITE HAS: Tent pad, picnic table, grill

WHEELCHAIR ACCESS: Yes

ASSIGNMENT: First come, first served and by
reservation (877-722-6762; ncparks.gov
/make-reservation)

REGISTRATION: Ranger will come by to
register you

AMENITIES: Water, flush toilets

PARKING: At tent campers' parking area only

FEE: $23

ELEVATION: 6,320'

RESTRICTIONS:

PETS: On 6' or shorter leash

FIRES: In fire grates only

ALCOHOL: Not allowed

OTHER: 14-day stay limit; no gathering of
firewood in the park; gates closed
6–10 p.m. (depending on season) to 7 a.m.

Sites 1 and 9 are the most private, but you'll feel lucky to get a site at all during summer weekends. This tiny campground exudes an intimate, secluded feel. The only noise you'll hear is the wind whipping over your head. By the way, Mount Mitchell is covered in fog, rain, or snow 8 out of every 10 days. Snow has been recorded every month of the year; 104 inches fall annually. Don't let those facts deter you, though—weather is part of the phenomenon that is Mount Mitchell.

The fog rolled in and out of the campground during my midsummer trip. Now and then the sun would shine, warming me. Wooded ridges came in and out of view with the fog; the whole scene seemed like some other world.

Carry a jacket along when you tramp through the park. First drive up to the summit parking area, and make the short jaunt to the observation tower atop Mount Mitchell. Here lie the remains of Elisha Mitchell, who fell to his death from a waterfall after measuring the height of the mountain. From the tower you can see the Black Mountain Range and beyond. Back near the parking area, check out the museum that details the natural history of Mount Mitchell.

Many hiking trails thread the park. From the campground you can walk to the observation tower and connect to the Deep Gap Trail; it's a rugged 6-mile hike along the Black Mountain Range to several

Blooming rhododendrons line one of the park's trails.

peaks that stand more than 6,000 feet high. Or you can leave the campground on the Old Mount Mitchell Trail past the park restaurant and loop around Mount Hallback to return.

Mount Mitchell State Park is surrounded by the Pisgah National Forest, which is bisected by the Blue Ridge Parkway. This, in essence, increases the accessible forest area beyond the 1,860-acre state park. Many national forest trails connect to the state park trails, allowing nearly unlimited hiking opportunities. Procure a trail map from the park office for the best hiking experience.

Get your supplies in Asheville before you leave. Also check for the latest road conditions on the Blue Ridge Parkway at nps.gov/blri because you must drive the scenic road to reach the state park. The parkway makes for a scenic drive, but once in the highlands of the Black Mountains, you won't want to leave this wonderful mountaintop and campground.

Mount Mitchell State Park Campground

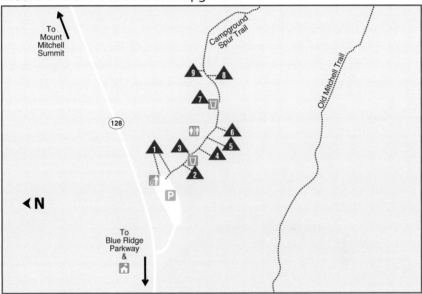

GETTING THERE

From Asheville, North Carolina, take the Blue Ridge Parkway north 27 miles to milepost 355. Turn left on NC 128 to enter Mount Mitchell State Park. The campground is 3.5 miles up the road on your right. The campground's address is 2388 NC 128, Burnsville, NC 28714.

GPS COORDINATES: N35° 45.458'   W82° 16.338'

11

Mount Pisgah Campground

Beauty ★★★★★ Privacy ★★★★ Spaciousness ★★★ Quiet ★★★★ Security ★★★★ Cleanliness ★★★★

Loops exclusively for tent campers complement the natural beauty of this nearly mile-high campground.

This is the highest campground on the entire Blue Ridge Parkway at nearly 5,000 feet. And that is just the beginning of the superlatives here. Try secluded sites just for tent campers in a high-country forest, complete with stately spruce trees. How about nature trails circling the campground? Throw in some hot showers at the comfort stations. Add some fantastic views along the parkway, and you have a great tent-camping destination.

The campground is wonderfully integrated into the mountain landscape of greater Mount Pisgah, specifically just below Flat Laurel Gap, amid the headwaters of Pisgah Creek and the 85-acre Flat Laurel bog, a rare high-country wetland where wind-sculpted birch and maple trees shade the campsites. Rhododendron and mountain laurel grow in dense thickets that offer plenty of privacy. Evergreens tower above all other vegetation. In this woodland, four

Mount Pisgah before leaf out

KEY INFORMATION

CONTACT: Blue Ridge Parkway, 828-298-0398; nps.gov/blri

OPEN: Mid-May–late October

SITES: 66 tent-only, 29 pop-up and van sites, 32 RV sites

EACH SITE HAS: Picnic table, fire grate, lantern post; some have tent pads

WHEELCHAIR ACCESS: Yes

ASSIGNMENT: First come, first served and by reservation (877-444-6777; recreation.gov)

REGISTRATION: At campground kiosk

AMENITIES: Hot showers, water spigots, flush toilets

PARKING: At campsites only; 2 vehicles/site

FEE: $20

ELEVATION: 4,980'

RESTRICTIONS:

PETS: On leash only

FIRES: In fire rings only

ALCOHOL: At campsites only

OTHER: 6 people/site; 30-day total stay limit in calendar year across all Blue Ridge Parkway campgrounds; 30' trailer-length limit; food (and dishes and utensils) must be stored in vehicle when not in use; only certified heat-treated firewood allowed; quiet hours 10 p.m.–6 a.m.

different loops put like-minded campers together. Loop A is for RVs but is little used by RVs or tent campers. Loop B is for pop-ups and campers, so it doesn't have tent pads, and the sites are less level than Loops C and D. Loop B has hot showers, as does Loop C.

Loops C and D are designated tent-camping loops, with 32 and 36 sites, respectively. Their tent sites are cut out of the forest, with heavy vegetation between them. Sometimes steps lead up or down to the sites from the paved auto pull-ins. If you have to look for a complaint, the sites are a tad small, and a few in C are a little close to the parkway. Overall, the sites are well maintained and well groomed, which adds to the already beautiful natural scenery.

Campsites are available without reservations any time except the major summer holiday weekends, but reservations can be made at any time. A campground host keeps things safe and orderly. Be apprised that food-storage regulations are in effect as a safeguard against bears. Because this campground is high, be prepared for cool conditions whenever you come. Bring a tarp to create a dry haven in case of rain.

The Blue Ridge Parkway sets the tone for Mount Pisgah, and you will enjoy great scenery on the way in. Once at the campground, you can enjoy walking some of the nature trails that form a network through and around the campground. Head to the tower atop Frying Pan Mountain, or loop over to Buck Spring Gap, and then walk to the top of Mount Pisgah, at 5,721 feet.

Not enough hiking opportunities? Why don't you visit Shining Rock Wilderness, just a few miles south on the Blue Ridge Parkway? I've enjoyed trekking here among the open fields, rock outcrops, and forests of this high-country preserve. Middle Prong Wilderness is less visited, more remote, and more wooded. Yellowstone Prong, a stream near Graveyard Fields Overlook south of the campground, has loop trails leading to three different falls, all relatively close together. The Cradle of Forestry Visitor Center is just a few miles down US 276 toward Brevard; see where the science of forestry began and explore some of the nature trails here. If you want to get wet, head down to Sliding Rock, a water feature on Looking Glass Creek where people shoot down a natural water slide into a pool. It's fun if you've never done it. Finally, the Mountains-to-Sea Trail traverses more miles along this area of the parkway than most hikers want to cover. A trail map of the Pisgah District of the Pisgah National Forest, which surrounds the parkway, comes in very handy here.

From the campground, a trail leads to the camp store, which sells some supplies and is near the Pisgah Inn on the other side of the parkway from Mount Pisgah. The inn serves breakfast, lunch, and dinner in case you don't feel like cooking. And you may be too tired to cook after all the hiking around here.

Mount Pisgah Campground

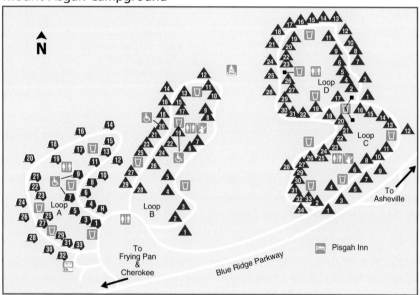

GETTING THERE

From Asheville, North Carolina, take I-26 to Exit 33 for NC 191. Take NC 191 S for 2.4 miles to the Blue Ridge Parkway; then turn south and take the parkway 15.2 miles to milepost 408.8. The campground will be on your right.

GPS COORDINATES: N35° 24.282'   W82° 45.398'

12

New River State Park:

WAGONER ACCESS CAMPGROUND

Beauty ★★★★ Privacy ★★★★ Spaciousness ★★★★ Quiet ★★★★★ Security ★★★★ Cleanliness ★★★★

The Wagoner Access tent campground on the banks of the New River is one of the best in the state.

North Carolina is blessed with many rivers, some of which are so exceptional as to receive wild and scenic designation. The New River is one of these. Located in the most north-westerly portion of the state, the New River courses through the mountains, northbound for Virginia. The state of North Carolina has long recognized the New River's beauty and works to protect this natural treasure while making it accessible, with paddler access points and campgrounds such as the Wagoner Access camping area of New River State Park. The riverside sites are all walk-in—or boat-in if you are traveling overnight down the river. No matter how you arrive, you will agree that this tent campground situated on the banks of the New is one of the best in the state.

Leave the walk-in parking area and cross a mown field, passing the remains of an old homestead with the chimney still standing. Reach campsite 49, sitting all alone in a small flat beside the spring run of the old homesite. Beyond here, the forest is regenerating in formerly plowed fields. A mix of black walnut, locust, and tulip trees shades the area amid thick brush. Mown paths reach the sites. Campsite 50 has its own path to a riverside site but has limited shade. Site 48 is circled by brush and shaded by cherry trees. Cross a little wet-weather stream to enter the rest of the campground. Site 47 is directly along the river and is shaded by walnut trees. Site 46 is also along the river, but a steep bank prevents direct river access—the campground operates its own river landing, and park personnel encourage using only this access to keep down erosion. Site 45 is adjacent to campsite 46.

Aerial view of the New River

courtesy of the North Carolina Division of Parks and Recreation

KEY INFORMATION

CONTACT: 336-982-2587; ncparks.gov /new-river-state-park

OPEN: March–November

SITES: 11

EACH SITE HAS: Picnic table, fire grate, trash can

WHEELCHAIR ACCESS: No

ASSIGNMENT: First come, first served and by reservation (877-722-6762; ncparks.gov /make-reservation)

REGISTRATION: Ranger will come by to register you

AMENITIES: Hot showers, water spigots, flush toilets

PARKING: At lot below ranger station

FEE: $9

ELEVATION: 2,600'

RESTRICTIONS:

PETS: On leash only

FIRES: In fire rings only

ALCOHOL: Prohibited

OTHER: 14-day stay limit in a 30-day period; gates closed 8–10 p.m. (depending on season) to 7 a.m.

Site 44 is on a slight slope, but landscaping timbers have been added to level it beneath crabapple trees. Site 43 is closest to the bathhouse, which is heated in the cooler months. Shaded by tulip trees and located beside the campground's river access, site 42 is the most popular, especially with boat-in campers. Site 41 is also near the boat access but is farther into the woods and is heavily shaded. Campsite 40 is well shaded by pines.

This campground at the Wagoner Access fills on holiday weekends only. It can get a little busy at the beginning and end of summer. Sites are always available on weekdays. Critters such as raccoons abound in this area, so secure your food while camping here. Just so you know, New River State Park also has a camping area at the US 221 Access, 11 river miles distant from the Wagoner Access.

Most folks who camp here like to paddle the river, but even if you're not a boater, you can still have a good time. The mile-plus Fern Nature Trail circles the valley beside the campground. Add a mile and connect with the Running Cedar Trail. A pretty picnic area, once an apple orchard, lies adjacent to the camping area. The trees still produce fruit, attracting deer and humans alike in fall. A rapid drops just above the campground access, offering fishing opportunities and a decent little swimming hole below it. A large field below the parking area affords room for games and general running around.

But face it: this park was developed with the paddler in mind. The state manages 26 miles of river here and maintains several access points for day and overnight trips. A popular run here is from the NC 88 bridge down to Wagoner Access, 5 miles in length. From Wagoner Access to the US 221 Access is 11 miles; plan for an all-day trip. Paddling times vary with river flows and weather conditions. Also, trips run slower if you like to fish your way downriver, as I do. Angling here is good for smallmouth bass, rock bass, and bream. Determined anglers might land a muskie.

An outfitter is located nearby if you are boatless or just want a shuttle. Zaloo's Canoes offers inner tubes for fun, canoes and kayaks for rent, and shuttle services of varying lengths. Reservations are required. For more information, call 800-535-4027 or visit zaloos .com. The river scenery is both mountainous and pastoral, deserving of its wild and scenic status. Rapids are mild, not exceeding Class 2, making the New a great training river. After you enjoy the Wagoner Access on the river, you'll want to check out other state park access areas that lie along this preserved water in North Carolina's northwest corner.

New River State Park: Wagoner Access Campground

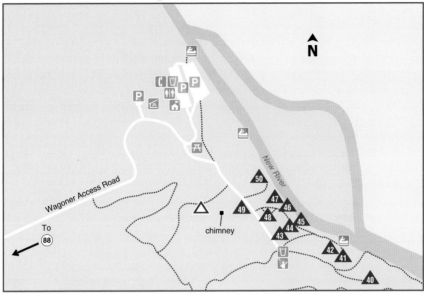

GETTING THERE

From the junction with US 421 on the west side of Wilkesboro, North Carolina, take NC 16 north 22.9 miles to NC 88. Turn right, heading east on NC 88, and follow it 1.4 miles to Wagoner Access Road. Turn left on Wagoner Access Road, and follow it 1 mile to enter the park. The park's address is 358 New River State Park Road, Laurel Springs, NC 28644.

GPS COORDINATES: N36° 24.912' W81° 23.142'

North Mills River Campground

Beauty ★★★ Privacy ★★★★ Spaciousness ★★★ Quiet ★★★★ Security ★★★★★ Cleanliness ★★★★

This unhurried, family-atmosphere campground rarely fills to capacity.

North Mills River Campground lies on the very edge of the Pisgah National Forest. But you would never know it by the sylvan setting of the area, divided by the free-flowing North Mills River, which has cut a valley amid the Carolina mountains. All roads leading to and within the campground are paved, which lures in a few extra RVers. This unhurried, family-atmosphere campground rarely fills to capacity.

As you approach the campground, it seems much larger than it really is, due to the sizable picnic area adjacent to the campground. To your right is a half-moon-shaped camping loop containing 13 campsites. These sites lie in a very level area between the North Mills River and a steep hill. Tall shade trees grow high over the grassy understory. The five sites inside the half-moon are spread far apart and are mostly open. These sites are for the campers with excess gear who don't mind a slight sacrifice in privacy. Some sites on the outskirts of the loop are set into the hillside. The campground host resides on this loop. Four water spigots are evenly spaced among the campsites. A comfort station with flush toilets is at the loop's center.

This alluring waterway is the main highlight of this camping experience.

KEY INFORMATION

CONTACT: Pisgah Ranger District, Pisgah National Forest, 828-890-3284; www.fs.usda.gov/recarea/nfsnc/recarea/?recid=48114

OPEN: Year-round (November–March: limited services)

SITES: 23, 1 full hook-up site

EACH SITE HAS: Tent pad, picnic table, fire ring; site 14 has full hookup

WHEELCHAIR ACCESS: Yes

ASSIGNMENT: First come, first served and by reservation (877-444-6777; recreation.gov)

REGISTRATION: Self-registration

AMENITIES: Hot showers, water spigot, flush toilets, waterless toilet

PARKING: At campsites only; 2 vehicles/site ($3/additional vehicle)

FEE: $22; $31 full hookup

ELEVATION: 2,500'

RESTRICTIONS:

PETS: On leash only

FIRES: In fire grates only

ALCOHOL: At campsites only

OTHER: 2 tents/site; 14-day stay limit

The main campground loop is across a bridge over the North Mills River. These 12 sites are on a slight slope declining toward the river. As you drive along the one-way road, look for a field inside the loop. Four spacious and open sites are set in the field. A short spur road dead-ends off this loop and leads to three smaller campsites; this trio offers the most isolation in the entire campground.

As you continue along the main loop, the field gives way to an understory of hemlock, fern, and rhododendron growing among nearly hidden campsites. This understory grows very thick, especially as the loop parallels the river. Three single sites and one double site are located riverside beneath tall evergreens. Four water spigots are situated along the loop. A lighted bathroom lies in the dark, forested center of the loop.

North Mills River is used mostly by local families. Children float down the river in inner tubes, and anglers fish for trout, while others explore the nearby forest trails. As summer evenings darken and cool down, campers often meander from site to site and get to know their neighbors. Don't be surprised if you are paid a friendly visit and offered a cup of coffee by your fellow camper. The campground host is often the center of these social gatherings.

To get a good lay of the land combined with a little history, take a scenic forest drive. Gravel Forest Service Road 1206 leaves the campground just beyond the self-service pay station. It will lead you to the Pink Beds Visitor Center. The Pink Beds is a 6,800-acre mountain valley where professional forestry was first practiced in the United States. It is a National Historic Site complete with a museum that tells of the evolution of forestry in our country. Two interpretive trails enhance the story of George Vanderbilt's management of his forestland. This valley is also known as the Cradle of Forestry in America.

To complete your scenic drive, turn right on US 276 from the Pink Beds and intersect the Blue Ridge Parkway after 3.8 miles. The Blue Ridge Parkway extends 469 miles to link the Great Smoky Mountains and Shenandoah National Parks. Head north on the parkway and enjoy some of the scenery for which this road is known. Stop and climb the 1-mile Frying Pan Mountain Trail to the lookout tower at its peak. Farther north is your right turn back onto gravel FS 479 and back down to the Mills River Recreation Area.

Informal hiking and fishing trails fan out from the campground. Several marked trails start 2 miles from the campground up FS 479 just after its junction with FS 142. The Big

Creek Trail (#102) and Trace Ridge Trail (#354) are two trails of note. They both leave the North Mills River watershed to intersect the Blue Ridge Parkway and the high country. If you're not sure exactly where to go, just ask your neighbor. Most local folks in the campground will gladly steer you onto a nearby good path. After all, they're quite proud of their mountain lands.

North Mills River Campground

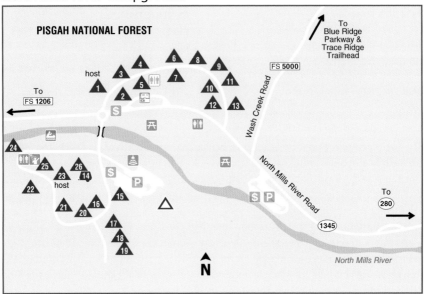

GETTING THERE

From Exit 40 on I-26, south of Asheville, North Carolina (near the airport), head south on NC 280 W for 3.8 miles. Turn right on North Mills River Road/NC 1345 at the campground sign, and follow North Mills River Road 5.1 miles, intersecting the North Mills River Campground. The park address is 5289 North Mills River Road, Mills River, NC 28742.

GPS COORDINATES: N35° 24.423'   W82° 38.741'

Rocky Bluff Campground

Beauty ★★★★ Privacy ★★★ Spaciousness ★★★ Quiet ★★★★ Security ★★★ Cleanliness ★★★★

The design of this campground will capture your fancy, and the setting will make you stay.

As I headed down into the Rocky Bluff Recreation Area, I found it hard to believe that there was a campground there. The road dipped into hilly terrain, with nary a flat spot to be found. But soon enough, there was the beginning of Rocky Bluff Campground. *Engineering marvel* may be a stretch, but a ton or two of site leveling and stonework were necessary to fit this campground into the wooded dips and rises of the land. All that stonework makes your back ache just looking at it.

Rocky Bluff Campground is divided into two loops. Enter the lower loop as you pass the pay station. Three shaded sites are dug into the hillside and reinforced with the above-mentioned stonework. Five open sites sit on the inside of the loop, on what passes for flat ground here at Rocky Bluff.

A view down to the French Broad River near Hot Springs

KEY INFORMATION

CONTACT: Appalachian Ranger District, Pisgah National Forest, 828-689-9694; www.fs.usda.gov/recarea/nfsnc /recarea/?recid=48114

OPEN: Memorial Day weekend–Labor Day

SITES: 29

EACH SITE HAS: Tent pad, picnic table, fire grate, lantern post

WHEELCHAIR ACCESS: Yes

ASSIGNMENT: First come, first served; no reservations

REGISTRATION: Self-registration

AMENITIES: Water, flush toilets

PARKING: At campsites only

FEE: $8

ELEVATION: 1,780'

RESTRICTIONS:

PETS: On 6' or shorter leash

FIRES: In fire grates only

ALCOHOL: At campsites only

OTHER: 14-day stay limit; 18' trailer-length limit

At the low point of the lower loop, a road spurs off to the right and leads to the upper loop. As the road makes a steep climb, two campsites are somehow fit into the terrain. Seven sites lie on top of the hill, spread along the road as it makes a short loop to return to the main campground. Two sites offer a view into Spring Creek hollow to the east.

A warning to those who get spooked easily: Also atop this hill, right next to the campsites, is Brooks Cemetery. Three sites look on to it. Stay down on the lower loop if the proximity of the cemetery will prevent you from enjoying a sound night's sleep.

Intersect the lower loop again from the upper-loop road. Here, sites are strewn in the open, lightly wooded center of the loop; a few more are tucked away in the thickets outside the loop. There isn't a whole lot of privacy. Due to the sloping terrain, you are probably going to be looking down on another camper or vice versa. A generally grassy understory doesn't shield you much from your neighbor, either. The upper loop, where ironically you might want to keep your neighbor in view to make sure he isn't a ghost roaming from the cemetery, is more wooded.

The lower-loop road passes a picnic area on the right and returns to the pay station. This loop has the only comfort station for the 30-site campground. Those on the upper loop must walk down the hill to use the facilities. But water spigots are conveniently placed around both loops for your convenience.

The terrain and stonework make this campground unique, and the cemetery adds a touch of history and mystique. If the cemetery isn't enough of the past, imagine this place a century ago when there was a community of homes, a blacksmith shop, and a school.

The nearest community, Hot Springs, embodies small-town Appalachia. It's full of nice people who work hard for a living in the splendor of a land that is now more precious to them than ever before. The Appalachian Trail runs right through town. Visit the Pisgah National Forest Visitor Center, and check out the hot springs for which the community was named.

Outdoor pastimes are plentiful. Several outfitters in town will arrange a whitewater-rafting trip down the French Broad River, which flows through Hot Springs. A 6-mile biking trail runs along the river to Paint Rock, which marks the Tennessee–North Carolina state line. This dividing line crosses the bridge over the French Broad from Hot Springs. The Appalachian Trail crosses this bridge too. From here, make the short but rewarding climb to Lovers Leap. Then soothe your muscles in the actual hot springs, but you must pay for the privilege.

Two fulfilling trails depart from Rocky Bluff Campground. The 1.2-mile Spring Creek Nature Trail loops down to Spring Creek and follows it a good way before veering north and intersecting the campground again, making for a rewarding and short day hike. The Van Cliff Loop Trail is a little longer and tougher. It leaves the campground and climbs, crossing NC 209 on the way and hooking up into some piney woods before returning to the campground after 2.6 miles.

Rocky Bluff Campground

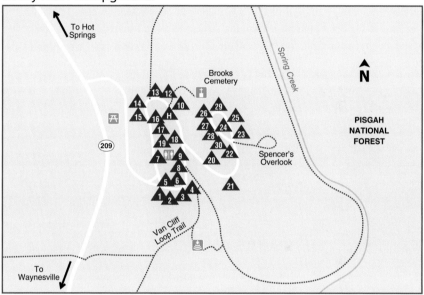

GETTING THERE

From the intersection of US 25 and NC 209 in Hot Springs, North Carolina, take NC 209 south 3.2 miles. Rocky Bluff Campground will be on your left.

GPS COORDINATES: N35° 51.845'   W82° 50.832'

15

Smokemont Campground

Beauty ★★★★ Privacy ★★ Spaciousness ★★★ Quiet ★★★ Security ★★★★★ Cleanliness ★★★★

Enjoy the Carolina side of the Smokies while conveniently located near the town of Cherokee.

Smokemont is strategically located on the Oconaluftee River at the base of the Smoky Mountains. From this location, campers can enjoy the immediate beauty of Great Smoky Mountains National Park and jump onto Newfound Gap Road northbound to explore other segments of the park. Take Newfound Gap Road just a few miles south, and you are in the tourist town of Cherokee. And if that isn't enough, you can take a ride on the Blue Ridge Parkway, which has just come 400-plus miles from Shenandoah National Park in Virginia to end near Smokemont. But this campground, nestled in a flat along Bradley Fork near the Oconaluftee River, exudes an old-time national-park camping atmosphere that may keep you mostly at your campsite, poking a stick into the fire, watching the trees grow, or listening to the water flow.

Bradley Fork flows beside the Smokemont Campground.

KEY INFORMATION

CONTACT: Great Smoky Mountains National Park, 865-436-1200; nps.gov/grsm

OPEN: Year-round

SITES: 98, 42 RV sites

EACH SITE HAS: Picnic table, fire grate, lantern post; some have tent pads

WHEELCHAIR ACCESS: Yes

ASSIGNMENT: First come, first served and by reservation May 15–October 31 (877-444-6777; recreation.gov)

REGISTRATION: At campground entrance station

AMENITIES: Water spigots, flush toilets

PARKING: At campsites only; 2 vehicles/site

FEE: $21–$25, depending on season

ELEVATION: 2,200'

RESTRICTIONS:

PETS: On 6' leash only

FIRES: In fire rings only

ALCOHOL: At campsites only

OTHER: 6 people/site; 14-day stay limit; 35' trailer-length limit; 40' RV-length limit; food (and dishes and utensils) must be stored in vehicle when not in use; only certified heat-treated firewood allowed; quiet hours 10 p.m.–6 a.m.

The campground is much longer than wide, stretching up the hollow of Bradley Fork, a fine, clear mountain stream that serenades the entire campground. Pass the ranger station and campground office. Campsites are strung out in loop form beneath the shade of oaks, maples, dogwoods, and hemlocks. The first loops, A and B, are open year-round, whereas C, D, and F (the RV loops) may be closed in colder times.

Overall, the sites are on the small side, and a lack of brush between campsites limits privacy. Strategically placed river boulders keep cars and campers separated. Old stone outbuildings house the bathrooms and also have outdoor sinks on them for washing dishes. Continue up the hollow to reach D Loop, which has more hemlocks. The sites are situated three wide here; the ones in the middle have less privacy. Shade is extensive throughout the campground and will be welcome in summer. Loop F is across Bradley Fork.

Summer is the busy time. Reservations are available between May 15 and October 31, so make them if you can. Campsites are available the rest of the year, and people do camp here year-round, even in the depths of winter. A word to the wise: store your food properly here—this is bear country, after all, and it's a park regulation.

Simply being in the Smoky Mountains is the attraction. There is so much to see in the park. However, there is plenty to do right here in Smokemont, especially hiking. The Smokemont Loop Trail leads along Bradley Fork, then upward along the southern reaches of Richland Mountain and past the Bradley Cemetery, returning to the campground after 5 miles. The Bradley Fork Trail heads toward Cabin Flats, a backcountry campsite that makes a great day-hiking destination along upper Bradley Fork. If you are feeling aggressive, make a loop using Chasteen Creek Trail and head to the high country along Hughes Ridge; then return via Bradley Fork, a good trout-fishing stream. Speaking of fishing, here's a tip—the farther you get from the campground, the better the fishing. Oconaluftee River offers roadside trout angling. Or you can head up Big Cove Road or down into Cherokee for some ramped-up put-and-take fishing on American Indian reservation lands. The waters of the Smokies are not just for fishing, however. The cool streams are also good for a summer dip or even tubing. Be careful of slippery rocks and strong currents, though.

As previously mentioned, the Blue Ridge Parkway is good for an auto tour, or you can head up Newfound Gap Road and then onward to Clingmans Dome, the highest point in the park at 6,642 feet. It has a tower for observation. Stop for a visit at the park's Oconaluftee Visitor Center and see the pioneer buildings.

If you want a little touristy fun, head down to Cherokee, where you can buy some moccasins, get some taffy, or gamble at the reservation casino. If you're feeling cultural, check out the outdoor drama *Unto These Hills,* which is held nightly. Arts and crafts abound in town as well. For more info, check out visitcherokeenc.com. Just remember that you have some camping to do, too, at Smokemont.

Smokemont Campground

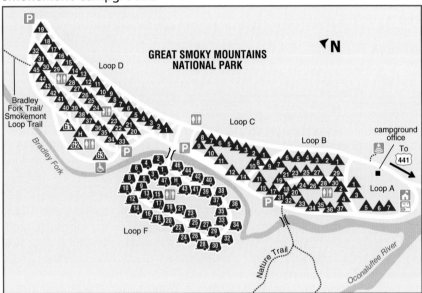

GETTING THERE

From the intersection of US 441 and US 19 near the Oconaluftee River in Cherokee, North Carolina, take US 441 N for 6.7 miles. Turn right on Smokemont Road, and immediately turn left after crossing the river to reach the campground.

GPS COORDINATES: N35° 33.432'   W83° 18.718'

16

South Mountains State Park Campground

Beauty ★★★★★ Privacy ★★★ Spaciousness ★★★ Quiet ★★★★ Security ★★★★★ Cleanliness ★★★★

Tent campers will love this rugged backwoods state park with an emphasis on wilderness.

During my roaming while writing this book, park rangers and others kept mentioning South Mountains State Park as an ideal candidate for inclusion here. By the time I got to the park, my expectations were as high as an Appalachian peak. And my trip here was as satisfying as a view from such a high place. South Mountains State Park delivers in both its small, rustic streamside campground and its 18,000 acres of wilderness to explore. This is a wilderness park—nothing but you and nature. After you set up camp, your exploration can be a day trip by foot or mountain bike, or a backpack for those inclined to overnight in the backcountry. Many visitors mix up a trip, first camping in the campground, then setting off into the backcountry. The park's amenities have been carefully integrated into the South Mountains, an outlier range far from the more-popular peaks straddling the North Carolina–Tennessee border.

High Shoals Falls
courtesy of North Carolina Division of Parks and Recreation

The 18-site campground is set in a flat along Jacob Fork, a crystalline, musical trout stream that tumbles over gray rocks and resonates among the campsites. Immediately reach campsite 1, where landscaping timbers delineate each site and corral small gravel within the tent pads for drainage. Each site's fittings, that is, picnic tables and lantern posts, are in fine condition. Tall, straight tulip trees and white pines shade the campground, along with hemlock, sourwood, hickory, maple, and sweet gum. Site 2 is across the campground road from Jacob Fork. Sites 3 and 4 are near the creek and back up against mountain laurel and rhododendron. More sites are set directly along the creek. Site 7 is a wheelchair-accessible site and has a wide picnic table. Site 8 has many hemlocks overhead. I wish I had stayed in site 9, which backs directly against the stream and overlooks a steep hillside. Site 10 is also beside Jacob Fork. Unfortunately, I arrived just at dark and didn't want to bother other campers by driving through the campground

KEY INFORMATION

CONTACT: 828-433-4772; ncparks.gov
/south-mountains-state-park

OPEN: Year-round

SITES: 18

EACH SITE HAS: Picnic table, fire ring, lantern post, tent pad; 3 have electricity

WHEELCHAIR ACCESS: Yes

ASSIGNMENT: First come, first served and by reservation (877-722-6762; ncparks.gov
/make-reservation)

REGISTRATION: Stop by visitor center first, or ranger will register you

AMENITIES: Hot showers, water spigots, flush toilets

PARKING: At campsites only; 2 vehicles/site

FEE: $15–$23; $18–$28 electric

ELEVATION: 1,350'

RESTRICTIONS:

PETS: On leash only

FIRES: In fire rings only

ALCOHOL: Prohibited

OTHER: 14-day stay limit; gates closed 7–10 p.m. (depending on season) to 7 a.m.

---

multiple times, even though I normally "loop the loop" before choosing a site. Site 11 was my choice. The next seven campsites were added later, along with the bathhouse featuring hot showers, across from site 11. Site 12 is wheelchair accessible and is one of three sites here with electricity. Site 13 is set well back in the woods. Campsites 14 and 15 back up to Jacob Fork. Campsite 16 is big and private. Campsites 17 and 18 are pull-through sites with electricity, designed for RVs.

I enjoyed being deep in this mountain valley. So do others, as the small campground fills most summer weekends; I recommend fall or spring, when it's wide open. During spring the wildflowers will be blooming and the creeks running high, which makes the many waterfalls and cascades more enticing. In fall, the colors will be every bit as good as those in the main Appalachian Range, but less busy. Campers can get a site any time of year during the week.

The South Mountains range from 1,200 to around 3,000 feet high. That makes visiting them more appealing in spring and fall, as they will be less chilly than other, higher ranges. Alternately, summer can be warm but is not oppressively hot. The park has 40 miles of trails to explore, ranging from a 0.75-mile interpretive nature trail along Jacob Fork, very worth your time, to loops long enough for you to bring your sleeping bag should you attempt them. Popular day hikes lead to High Shoals Falls, which can be made into a loop hike, to Little River Falls, and to Jacob Knob Overlook. A good park-trail map reveals other loop possibilities. The many park streams offer trout fishing in an attractive setting. Not only does the park contain the entire Jacob Fork watershed, but it also has acquired the Clear Creek and Henry Fork drainages. Anglers are limited only by time and desire. Be apprised of the latest license requirements and fishing regulations before you strike out.

Mountain bikers have an 18-mile designated loop that the park deems strenuous, so be prepared for a long outing on this path, which circles the ridgelines along Jacob Creek—and bring your water bottle. After my experience at South Mountains State Park, I will be circling back to this place for more of the best in tent camping.

South Mountains State Park Campground

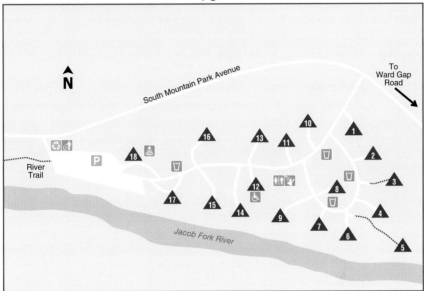

GETTING THERE

From Exit 105 on I-40 near Morganton, North Carolina, turn left to take NC 18 S for 10.8 miles. Turn right on Sugar Loaf Road, and follow it 4.2 miles; then turn left on Old NC 18. Go 2.6 miles; then turn right on NC 1901/Ward Gap Road, follow it 1.3 miles, and veer right onto South Mountain Park Avenue. Follow South Mountain Park Avenue 3.5 miles to reach the campground. The park's address is 3001 South Mountain State Park Ave., Connelly Springs, NC 28612.

GPS COORDINATES: N35° 35.825'   W81° 37.397'

17

Standing Indian Campground

Beauty ★★★★★ Privacy ★★★★ Spaciousness ★★★★★ Quiet ★★★ Security ★★★★ Cleanliness ★★★★

Soak in the mountains of the Standing Indian Basin from the headwaters of the Nantahala River.

According to Cherokee legend, a warrior was once posted on top of a certain mountain to look out for a flying monster that had snatched a child from a nearby village. The villagers prayed to the Great Spirit to annihilate the monster. A violent storm struck the mountain, reducing it to rock and turning the lookout warrior into a stone "standing Indian."

The Nantahala River is born on Standing Indian Mountain just upstream from this outstanding high-country campground, where cool breezes from the ridgetops temper the warm summer air. With sites on five loops, Standing Indian is spread out and offers a variety of site conditions. The first loop diffuses along the Nantahala with hemlock-shaded sites isolated by thick stands of rhododendron. Across the river, three loops are spread out in a large, flat area interspersed with large hardwoods that allow plenty of sun and grass to flourish among their ranks. Ritter Lumber Company once had a logging camp here. Farther back still, across Kimsey Creek, are mountainside sites. They stand level among the sloping forest of yellow birch, beech, and sugar maple, and are separated by lush greenery that makes each site seem isolated. Six double sites accommodate larger groups.

Big Laurel Falls is a great hike destination for Standing Indian tent campers.

KEY INFORMATION

CONTACT: Nantahala Ranger District, Nantahala National Forest, 828-524-6441; www.fs.usda.gov/recarea/nfsnc/recarea/?recid=48634

OPEN: April–October

SITES: 84

EACH SITE HAS: Tent pad, picnic table, fire grate, lantern post

WHEELCHAIR ACCESS: Yes

ASSIGNMENT: First come, first served and by reservation (877-444-6777; recreation.gov)

REGISTRATION: Self-registration

AMENITIES: Hot showers, water, flush toilets

PARKING: At campsites only

FEE: $16–$20

ELEVATION: 3,400'

RESTRICTIONS:

PETS: On a leash only

FIRES: In fire grates only

ALCOHOL: At campsites only

OTHER: 14-day stay limit; 21' trailer-length limit

Campground hosts occupy each loop for your safety and convenience. Sixteen water pumps are strategically located throughout the loops, in addition to five comfort stations with flush toilets (two of the comfort stations also have hot showers). There are no electric hookups. You may pick up dead, downed firewood from the surrounding area without a permit. Keep in mind that Standing Indian can be crowded during peak summer weekends.

There's plenty to do nearby. Try your luck at one of the campground horseshoe pits. Fish for trout on the Nantahala River or Kimsey Creek. Rainbow and brown trout are the predominant cold-water fish in the streams, with some brook trout in the upper waters. For the nonfishing water lover, there are two falls nearby. Drive 5 miles on Forest Service Road 67 beyond the turnoff to the campground. The Big Laurel Falls Trail sign is on the right. After passing over a footbridge, the trail splits. Veer to the right and come to Big Laurel Falls in 0.5 mile. The Mooney Falls Trail starts 0.7 mile beyond the Big Laurel Falls trailhead and leads 0.1 mile to the cascading falls.

Several trails begin at the campground. To orient yourself, find the Backcountry Information Center 0.2 mile left of the campground entrance gate. Study the map. Make an 8-mile loop out of the Park Creek and Park Ridge Trails. The Park Creek Trail starts at the Backcountry Information Center; follow it down the Nantahala, then up Park Creek to Park Gap. Take the Park Ridge Trail 3.2 miles back down to the campground. This hike is moderate to strenuous, with a net elevation change of 880 feet.

The most prominent trail in the area is the famed Appalachian Trail, which skirts the campground to the south and east. The 87-mile section extending from the Georgia line to the Smokies is considered by many hikers to be one of the most rugged sections, with its relentlessly steep ups and downs. This section weeds out many thru-hikers who aspire to "follow the white blaze" 2,100 miles to Maine.

The Appalachian Trail passes by FS 67 on the way to the campground. Drive out of the campground toward Wallace Gap about a mile. The Rock Gap parking area is on your right. Take the trail south (uphill to your right), and soon you'll come to the Rock Gap backcountry shelter, one of a series of shelters located about a day's walk from one another along the entirety of the trail. They provide a haven from the elements for the weary thru-hiker. Imagine this as your home for a six-month journey up the spine of the Appalachians.

While you're at Standing Indian Campground, why not see the mountain for which it was named? It's a strenuous 3.9-mile climb to the 5,499-foot peak, but the views provide ample reward. Use the Lower Ridge Trail, which starts on the left just beyond the campground bridge over the Nantahala. Switch back up to the ridge crest, and follow it southward to the Appalachian Trail. Take a spur trail 0.2 mile to the top of Standing Indian, and view the Blue Ridge Mountains and the Tallulah River Basin.

Standing Indian Campground

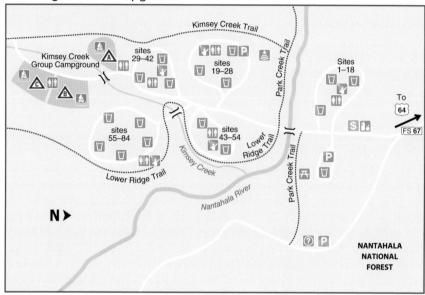

GETTING THERE

From the intersection of US 23 and US 64 in Franklin, North Carolina, drive west on US 64 for 11.9 miles. Following the sign to Standing Indian, turn left on West Old Murphy Road, and go 1.9 miles to Wallace Gap. Turn right at the sign on FS 67, and go 2 miles to the campground.

GPS COORDINATES: N35° 04.328'   W83° 31.850'

18

Sunburst Campground

Beauty ★★★ Privacy ★★★ Spaciousness ★★★ Quiet ★★★★ Security ★★★★ Cleanliness ★★★★

Sunburst lies at the base of two of North Carolina's best wildernesses.

Sunburst has an interesting name. It sounds like a high-dollar mountain resort, but the name is actually that of a logging town that was once here. Today, visitors see nothing but a small, appealing campground that lies at the base of two wilderness areas, Shining Rock and Middle Prong. If you explore the trails of the wildernesses, you may run into old iron implements of the logging era, especially in the Middle Prong, along with a rich forest replete with numerous wildflowers and clear mountain streams with native brook trout. Shining Rock offers open high-country meadows with far-reaching views. I have hiked both wildernesses and heartily endorse their beauty. So pack your tent, your hiking boots, and your energy, and then come on up to Sunburst.

Sunburst is the kind of campground that grows on you. At first sight, it seems a little small, but the beauty of the overall area is readily apparent. After all, you drive a Forest Heritage Scenic Byway to get here. The nine campsites are strung along a half loop across from the West Fork Pigeon River. The steep reaches of Beartrail Ridge form the campground backdrop. A large meadow lies between the river and the camping area, providing views of the tall ridges towering over Sunburst.

Enjoy scenery like this while hiking at Shining Rock Wilderness.

KEY INFORMATION

CONTACT: Pisgah Ranger District, Pisgah National Forest, 828-877-3265; www.fs.usda.gov/recarea/nfsnc /recarea/?recid=48114

OPEN: May–late October

SITES: 9

EACH SITE HAS: Tent pad, picnic table, fire grate, lantern post

WHEELCHAIR ACCESS: Yes

ASSIGNMENT: First come, first served; no reservations

REGISTRATION: Self-registration

AMENITIES: Water, flush toilet

PARKING: At campsites only; 2 vehicles/site; $3/additional vehicle; no parking on grass

FEE: $15

ELEVATION: 3,100'

RESTRICTIONS:

PETS: On leash only

FIRES: In fire grates only

ALCOHOL: At campsites only

OTHER: 8 people/site; 14-day stay limit within 30 days across all USFS campgrounds within 10 miles; quiet hours 10 p.m.–7 a.m.

The campsites, which lie between the gravel road and Beartrail Ridge, are adequately distant from one another. The U.S. Forest Service has landscaped between the campsites with spruce, rhododendron, and hardwoods for added privacy. A campground host is located in the center of the sites, adding safety, information, and security to Sunburst. The camp bathroom is up the hill behind the host. A small turnaround is at the far end of the camp, along with a picnic area for day visitors.

I have enjoyed Sunburst in three seasons, and it has never disappointed. Spring is the time of rebirth, and when on a fishing trip up nearby Middle Prong, I could hardly concentrate on my line because I was so distracted by wildflowers galore. Summertime found me up on the meadows and clearings of Shining Rock, looming over the high country of the Black Mountains, so named for the dark mantle of spruce and fir that cloaks their highest points (I have also been here during winter—cold and snowy!). My latest trip took place on a warm fall day, when I toured the area by auto, watching strong winds return the leaves from the hardwoods back to the earth.

A rewarding but long 11-mile hike in the Middle Prong Wilderness leaves Sunburst Campground and follows nearby Forest Service Road 97 up to the Haywood Gap Trail. Head up Middle Prong, then on up Haywood Stream to Haywood Gap and the Blue Ridge Parkway. Then take the Mountains-to-Sea Trail along the crest of Pisgah Ridge down to the Buckeye Gap Trail, returning to Middle Prong. The fishing is good on Middle Prong and the West Prong Pigeon River. West Prong also has some big water holes that invite a dip for sweaty hikers.

The easiest way to access Shining Rock Wilderness is to take NC 215 up to the Blue Ridge Parkway, then head north a short distance. Or you could take the Fork Mountain Trail and hike 6 miles and climb nearly 3,000 feet. I'd drive if I were you, then park below Black Balsam Knob, 6,214 feet. From here, take the Art Loeb Trail over Black Balsam Knob and Tennent Mountain. Keep on past Ivestor Gap and on to Shining Rock, where views await from atop white quartz outcrops. Return via the Ivestor Gap Trail for a loop of around 9 miles. Also nearby is Yellowstone Falls, off the Gravestone Fields Trail, and attractive falls along Laurel Creek on the Laurel Creek Trail. A map of the wildernesses is well worth its money and will keep you plenty busy on your trip to Sunburst.

Sunburst Campground

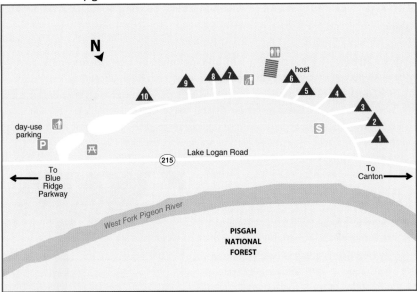

GETTING THERE

From Exit 31 on I-40 near Canton, North Carolina, take NC 215/Champion Drive south 1 mile, and turn right on NC 215/Blackwell Drive, crossing the Pigeon River. In 0.8 mile turn left on US 23, and go 0.4 mile. Turn right on Reed Street, and in 0.2 mile continue on NC 215. Go 2 miles and turn left to remain on NC 215. Drive 3.3 miles, and turn right to stay on NC 215. Go 0.3 mile, turn left on NC 215, and go 0.2 mile. Turn left on US 276, go 0.7 mile, and turn right on NC 215. In 9.5 miles Sunburst Campground will be on your right. The campground's address is 8820 Lake Logan Road, Canton, NC 28716.

GPS COORDINATES: N35° 22.273'   W82° 56.347'

Tsali Campground

Beauty ★★★★ Privacy ★★★ Spaciousness ★★★ Quiet ★★ Security ★★★★★ Cleanliness ★★★★★

Head straight from the tent and go mountain biking, boating, horseback riding, hiking, or fishing.

What do a Cherokee, a pioneer, a big dam, and mountain biking have in common? Answer: They have all played a major part in the evolution of Tsali Recreation Area.

In 1838, during a forced removal of American Indians to the West that became known as the Trail of Tears, a Cherokee leader by the name of Tsali sacrificed himself so other Cherokee could remain in the area. These natives formed the nucleus of the Eastern Band of Cherokee, who now live on a reservation adjacent to Bryson City.

Early in the 20th century, pioneers raised corn along Mouse Branch; there they turned grain into corn juice, otherwise known as moonshine. Now the plot is Tsali Campground, where hikers, paddlers, horseback riders, and especially mountain bikers congregate. These hearty adventurers catch their collective breath here at Tsali between excursions along the 39 miles of trails that emanate from the campground bordering Fontana Lake.

Tsali Campground is divided into two loops, an upper and a lower. The upper loop has 22 sites. The U.S. Forest Service keeps the campground well groomed, and plenty of second-growth hardwoods and pines shade the former field. A sparse understory makes the campground open yet sacrifices privacy. Six of the sites are spread along Mouse Branch. Four water spigots are evenly dispersed along the loop. In its center sit a pair of low-volume flush toilets.

The lower loop features 19 sites and is more open and spacious than the upper loop due to fewer trees and, in some spots, a grassy understory. Eight sites back up against Mouse Branch. At the head of the lower loop is a modern bath facility with flush toilets and hot showers, which are quite popular with sweaty hikers and mountain bikers.

Cast a line in Fontana Lake to catch walleye, muskie, or smallmouth bass.

KEY INFORMATION

CONTACT: Cheoah Ranger District, Nantahala National Forest, 828-479-6431; www.fs.usda.gov/recarea/nfsnc /recarea/?recid=48634

OPEN: April–October

SITES: 41

EACH SITE HAS: Tent pad, picnic table, fire grate, lantern post

WHEELCHAIR ACCESS: Yes

ASSIGNMENT: First come, first served; no reservations

REGISTRATION: Self-registration

AMENITIES: Hot showers, water, flush toilets

PARKING: At campsites only

FEE: $15

ELEVATION: 1,750'

RESTRICTIONS:

PETS: On leash only

FIRES: In fire rings only

ALCOHOL: At campsites only

OTHER: 14-day stay limit

Three water spigots are conveniently located on this loop, where a short trail leads down to Fontana Lake.

The campground is full on weekends and busy during the week with active campers. Mountain bikers from all over the Southeast converge on Tsali to ride its trails. Many campers also bring canoes and kayaks to drift on Fontana Lake and glide on the nearby whitewater rivers. Hikers abound; pleasure boaters and equestrians are represented too.

Tsali Recreation Area has four primary trails. The U.S. Forest Service has devised a system enabling hikers, mountain bikers, and equestrians to enjoy the trails without bothering one another. Hikers can use all four trails at any time. The Right Loop and Left Loop Trails are paired together. The Mouse Branch and Thompson Loop Trails are paired together in a system whereby equestrians and mountain bikers alternate using them daily. Right Loop Trail is a singletrack trail that extends for 11 miles with views of Fontana Lake. It can be shortened to 4- or 8-mile loops. The Left Loop Trail is a 12-mile, singletrack pathway that features an overlook with a view of the Smoky Mountains. Mouse Branch Trail mixes a singletrack trail with old logging roads and passes through old homesites along its 6-mile course. You may see wildlife on the 8-mile Thompson Loop Trail, which crosses streams and passes through wildlife openings and old homesites. Check the trail-use schedule posted at the campground.

The boat ramp presents more recreational opportunities. Sea kayakers love to ply the mountain-rimmed waters of Fontana Lake. You can fish in Fontana Lake or access the Smokies. Cross the water and anchor in any cove on the Smokies side of the lake. Then meander up the creek that created the cove, and you will run into the Lakeshore Trail, which runs for miles in both directions. Many relics of the past, including stone walls, chimneys, and broken china, may be seen. Make it an adventure. But remember, all artifacts are part of the recreation area and must be left behind for others to enjoy.

Other facilities at Tsali include a bike-washing area for cleaning up after those long, muddy rides; a stable for horses; and a bank-fishing trail near the boat launch for safely wetting a line. If you need supplies, drive 6 miles west on NC 28 to Wolf Creek General Store.

This is a fun area for active people. Use Tsali as a base camp, and enjoy all of the activities available in this beautiful section of the Southern Appalachians.

Tsali Campground

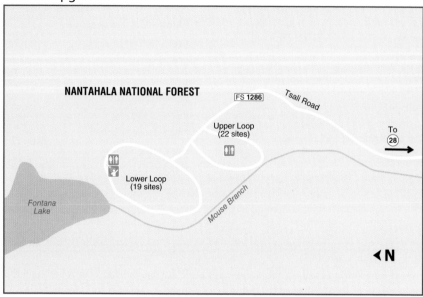

NANTAHALA NATIONAL FOREST

FS 1286

Tsali Road

Upper Loop
(22 sites)

To
28

Lower Loop
(19 sites)

Fontana
Lake

Mouse Branch

N

GETTING THERE

From Bryson City, North Carolina, take US 19 S for 3.1 miles, then turn right on US 74/ US 19, and go 5.2 miles. Turn right on NC 28 and go 3.5 miles. Turn right at the signed junction on FS 1286/Tsali Road, and follow it 1.5 miles. Tsali Campground will be on your left.

GPS COORDINATES: N35° 24.355'   W83° 35.195'

NORTH CAROLINA PIEDMONT

Tory Falls at Hanging Rock State Park *(see campground 21, page 73)*

20

Badin Lake Campground

Beauty ★★★ Privacy ★★★★ Spaciousness ★★★ Quiet ★★★★ Security ★★★★★ Cleanliness ★★★★

Badin Lake offers water and land recreation in the Uwharrie Mountains.

Depending on where you're coming from, there are several ways to reach Badin Lake Campground. Most of them take a lot of twists and turns, but the drive is worth it. This lakeside campground is the pride of the Uwharrie National Forest and is a best bet for tent campers who want a good campground accompanied by water and land recreation, including boating, fishing, and hiking. Maybe that's why it seems that all roads and signs in the Uwharrie National Forest lead to Badin Lake Campground, which has gotten a recent makeover and now includes hot showers and flush toilets in the bathhouses.

This lakeside camp is broken into two loops. The lower loop has campsites 1–22. The terrain slopes toward Badin Lake, but the sites themselves have been leveled with landscaping timbers. Some sites are multitiered. Pines reach high, with cedars, oaks, sweet gum, and heavy brush below. The lakeside sites start with 4. If you are reserving a site and want to camp by the lake, go for sites 4, 8, 9, 11, 12, or 13, which are singles. Sites 6 and 20 are double sites. The lower loop curves away from the lake and offers more-attractive, wooded sites.

Scenic hills rise from the waters of Badin Lake.

KEY INFORMATION

CONTACT: Uwharrie Ranger District, Uwharrie National Forest, 910-576-6391; www.fs.usda.gov/recarea/nfsnc /recarea/?recid=48934

OPEN: Year-round

SITES: 34

EACH SITE HAS: Tent pad, picnic table, fire grate, lantern post

WHEELCHAIR ACCESS: Yes

ASSIGNMENT: First come, first served and by reservation (877-444-6777; recreation.gov)

REGISTRATION: Self-registration

AMENITIES: Hot showers, water spigots, flush toilets

PARKING: At campsites only

FEE: $12

ELEVATION: 525'

RESTRICTIONS:

PETS: On leash only

FIRES: In fire rings only

ALCOHOL: Prohibited

OTHER: 14-day stay limit; 40' RV-length limit

On a hill overlooking the lake, the upper loop has sites 23–35. This loop is lesser used and offers the most solitude; being farther from Badin Lake makes it less popular. Sites 26 and 29 are closest to the water. All sites are reservable, so crowding isn't a concern if you plan ahead. The sites are generally large and appear to be well maintained. Site 28 is a double site. Heavy brush between sites offers more-than-adequate privacy. A campground host is on duty most of the year, providing an element of safety not found at unhosted campgrounds. Both loops have bathhouses with shower facilities.

Badin Lake, covering 5,350 acres, is an impoundment of the Yadkin River. The eastern shore of the lake borders the national forest and is where the campground is located. Favored fish are bluegill, crappie, largemouth bass, catfish, and stripers. Anglers will be using worms and crickets with a bobber in spring for bluegill. Get on a bed of these fish, and you are in for some fun. Bass will be moving according to season; try looking for them at rocky points or around submerged logs. Crappie generally will go for minnows. Stripers are large bass that can be caught on live shad or top-water lures. Catfish are bottom-feeders and will go for chicken livers or even a hot dog if the bait is kept on the lakebed with weights.

While others ski, swim (although no formal swimming area exists), and sun on the lake, campers with lakeside sites can enjoy the water directly from their tents. For those with boats, Cove Boat Ramp is 2 miles from Badin Lake Campground, near Arrowhead Campground. Badin Lake Campground has a fishing pier nearby if you are boatless. Campers can enjoy lakeside hiking directly from their sites. Badin Lake Trail leads north and south along the shore to a make a loop. Southbound hikers will reach Cove Boat Ramp and Arrowhead Campground after 2.2 miles. The path then returns through the woods to the lake, circling around a north point then curving south past Kings Mountain Point, which also has a fishing pier. If you leave north from Badin Lake Campground, it is only 0.5 mile to Kings Mountain Point. The entire loop is 5.5 miles. You can hike to a remote spot and fish from shore or just look for wildlife, especially birds. Look also for evidence of gold mining, such as pits and tailings. Just realize your richest find here will be your campsite at Badin Lake Campground.

Badin Lake Campground

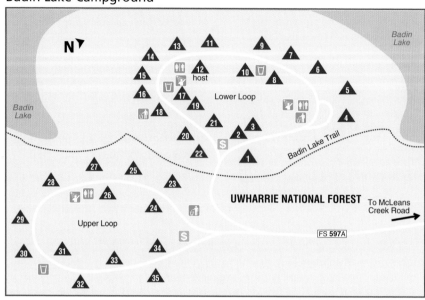

A shaded path beside Badin Lake

GETTING THERE

From the intersection of NC 134 and NC 27 in Troy, North Carolina, head east on NC 27/Albemarle Road, and go 0.1 mile. Turn right on West Spring Street, go 0.2 mile, and turn right on Bilhen Street, which becomes NC 109/Eldorado Street. Go 9.2 miles, and make a sharp left onto Reservation Road. Follow it 0.4 mile, then turn right on Moccasin Creek Road/Forest Service Road 576. Follow it 0.6 mile, then turn right on McLeans Creek Road/FS 544. Go 2.7 miles, and turn right on Badin Lake Road. Follow it 0.2 mile; then veer left on FS 597A and follow it 0.6 mile to the campground. All these turns are signed.

GPS COORDINATES:
N35° 26.862'   W80° 04.670'

21

Hanging Rock State Park Campground

Beauty ★★★★ Privacy ★★★ Spaciousness ★★ Quiet ★★★ Security ★★★★★ Cleanliness ★★★★

This state park is deservedly popular for its far-reaching vistas and tumbling cascades.

I can understand why Hanging Rock is so popular. The natural setting is dramatic: the Sauratown Mountains rise from the Piedmont in barren rock faces, forming natural vista points for overlooking the surrounding countryside. Hiking trails explore not only mountain lookouts but also waterfalls and woodlands. A ridge-rimmed lake with recreation opportunities offers a watery contrast to the land. Park facilities include a wood-and-stone bathhouse by the lake that is listed on the National Register of Historic Places. The lodgelike visitor center fits well in the setting and is full of interpretive information about the land, people, and history of this nearly 7,000-acre state park. Finally, the campground is an adequate jumping-off point for getting out and exploring this active camper's destination.

The campground at Hanging Rock is divided into two loops. The first loop has campsites 1–42 and is open throughout the week. Hickory, oak, and maple trees shade the ridgeline campground, which is slightly sloped. Sourwood, sassafras, and mountain laurel form a thick understory that screens the sites from one another. Sites are situated as the rocks

One of the many views from the high country at this fine state park

KEY INFORMATION

CONTACT: 336-593-8480; ncparks.gov
/hanging-rock-state-park

OPEN: Year-round (December–mid-March:
pit toilet only; bathhouse closed)

SITES: 73, 10 cabins

EACH SITE HAS: Tent pad, picnic table,
fire grate

WHEELCHAIR ACCESS: Yes

ASSIGNMENT: First come, first served and by
reservation (877-722-6762; ncparks.gov
/make-reservation); cabin reservations
required

REGISTRATION: Ranger will come by to
register you

AMENITIES: Hot shower, flush toilets,
water spigot

PARKING: At campsites only; must be on
parking pad

FEE: $15–$17; $10 in winter

ELEVATION: 1,500'

RESTRICTIONS:

PETS: On leash only

FIRES: In fire rings only

ALCOHOL: Prohibited

OTHER: 6 people and 2 tents/site; 14-day
stay limit in a 30-day period; gates closed
7–10 p.m. (depending on season) to 7 a.m.

and trees allow, resulting in sites of differing sizes and distances from the loop. A trail leads down to the park lake, which is in the valley below the campground.

The second loop, with sites 43–73, is stretched on a ridgeline road. The sites on the right side of the road are more desirable, as they face into the lake valley rather than toward the campground access road. Mountains are visible beyond the lake through the trees. The campground road descends along the ridge, but the sites themselves have been leveled. Be aware that these sites are closer together than those in the first loop.

Each loop has a bathhouse. Water spigots are adequately spread throughout the campground, which has a host to make your stay go more smoothly. The only real downside to this park is the popularity of the campground, which fills just about every nice weekend. However, making reservations can quell any concerns.

More than 18 miles of trails travel to and through the park's natural features. Hanging Rock Trail leads to the park's namesake. The area on the overhang is rugged and rocky! You can even see downtown Winston-Salem from here. Additional views await at other destinations. An observation tower, once a fire tower used by the state forest service, is at Moore's Knob, where many a passerby has inscribed his or her name in the rock bluff. Check out the vistas from Cook's Wall, which leads to a cliff edge and House Rock. Other worthwhile hiking destinations are the Lower Cascades, Upper Cascades, Window Falls, and Hidden Falls. Haven't gotten enough falls? Then head to Tory's Falls. Here also is Tory's Den, a cave that was purportedly used during the Revolutionary War.

The park lake has a rustic bathhouse built by the Civilian Conservation Corps (CCC) between 1935 and 1942. A slope leads beyond the bathhouse to a beach, then to the clear lake, which was dammed by the CCC. This attractive impoundment offers fishing from a pier. Visitors can also rent paddleboats and rowboats to tool around the lake or angle for bream and bass (no private boats are allowed, though). The impressive park visitor center has an interesting video from the CCC days, among other information that is worth discovering. As pretty as the park structures may be, the natural landscape is the star of the show here. Make time to pitch your tent, and check it out for yourself.

Hanging Rock State Park Campground

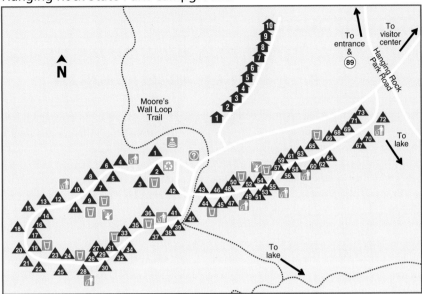

GETTING THERE

From Winston-Salem, North Carolina, take I-40 to Exit 193B and merge onto US 52 N. In 3 miles take Exit 110B, and head west on US 311 N for 17.4 miles. Keep straight on NC 89 W for 10.3 miles. Turn left on Hanging Rock Road, and follow it 1 mile to enter the state park. Continue another 2.3 miles to the campground on your right. The park's address is 1790 Hanging Rock Park Road, Danbury, NC 27016.

GPS COORDINATES: N36° 23.335'   W80° 16.690'

⛺ Lake Norman State Park Campground

Beauty ★★★ Privacy ★★★★ Spaciousness ★★ Quiet ★★ Security ★★★★★ Cleanliness ★★★

This state park offers the only publicly owned campground on Lake Norman.

With a name like Lake Norman, this state park is obviously a water-oriented destination. In that regard, it doesn't disappoint. Nearly the entire preserve is situated on a peninsula jutting into this impoundment, located just north of the greater Charlotte area. So it's no surprise that the park campground is by the water and that the park has a swim area, a boat launch, shore fishing, and a hiking trail that curves along the lake. If that's not enough water, there's more—Lake Norman State Park has its own small lake where you can rent canoes, paddleboats, kayaks, and paddleboards.

Once you arrive at the park, it seems to take forever to get to the actual campground. That is because the campground is at the tip of the peninsula that the state park owns. Having only 33 sites keeps the atmosphere relaxed even when the campground is full, which is just about every nice weekend between mid-April and Labor Day. Enter a loop with one crossroad cutting it in half. The peninsula is hilly enough to offer vertical variation, but the campsites have been leveled. A tent pad at each site ensures a level night's sleep. Many sites also have leveled picnic table pads, so the camp stew won't tip off your stove. A pretty forest

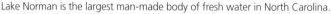

Lake Norman is the largest man-made body of fresh water in North Carolina.

KEY INFORMATION

CONTACT: 704-528-6350; ncparks.gov
/lake-norman-state-park

OPEN: Year-round

SITES: 32

EACH SITE HAS: Tent pad, picnic table,
fire ring; 1 with electricity

WHEELCHAIR ACCESS: Yes

ASSIGNMENT: First come, first served; and
by reservation (877-722-6762; ncparks.gov
/make-reservation)

REGISTRATION: Ranger will come by to
register you

AMENITIES: Hot showers, flush toilets,
water spigots

PARKING: At campsites only; must fit on
campsite pull-in

FEE: $15–$23; $23–$27 electric

ELEVATION: 800'

RESTRICTIONS:

PETS: On leash only

FIRES: In fire rings only

ALCOHOL: Prohibited

OTHER: 6 people/site; quiet hours 10 p.m.–
7 a.m.; gates closed 6–9 p.m. (depending
on season) to 7 a.m.

of cedar, shortleaf pine, sourwood, and other hardwoods shades the campground. The forest offers good campsite privacy.

Past the first three sites, the main campground road continues curving along the lakeshore while a crossroad turns left. A connector hiking trail leaves the campground to meet the Lakeshore Trail across from site 3. Sites 4, 5, and 6 are sloped downhill toward the lake and are heavily shaded. Site 12 is closest to the water, but none of the sites are directly lakeside. Sites 13 and 14 jut toward the water but are close to each other. The lake views are gone by site 20. Campsites 23 and 24 offer good solitude. The campground crossroad, on which the camp host stays, has sites 26–33, which are a bit packed in. Site 31 is near the bathhouse, which centers the loop and is convenient to all campers.

The campground is well maintained and appealing. Reservations

courtesy of North Carolina Division of Parks and Recreation

Lake Norman in fall

are strongly recommended during high summer. Weekdays aren't crowded, but the area does get some visitor traffic from I-77.

As mentioned earlier, this state park is centered on the water. The swim area on Lake Norman is popular during the summer. Boatless campers can fish from shore or head up to the small park lake; rent a paddleboat, kayak, or canoe; and fish in a no-gas-motors atmosphere. Those with boats will use the park's boat ramp to access Lake Norman for fishing, skiing, and general water recreation. If you want to be near the water but not on it, take the Lake Shore Trail. It meanders along most of the peninsula, which is bordered by Hicks Creek and the main lake. The entire loop is a 6.5-mile trek. Or take a shortcut on the Short Turn Trail and make your loop only 3.4 miles. The Alder Trail is much shorter, at 0.8 mile. It is located at the park lake, where the rental boats are. This used to be a busier area when the swim beach was here, but it now seems forgotten. Cyclists love to pedal along the many park roads. Mountain bikers have a 30.5-mile network of trails for those who want some off-road pedaling action. And there is plenty of outdoor action here at Lake Norman State Park.

Lake Norman State Park Campground

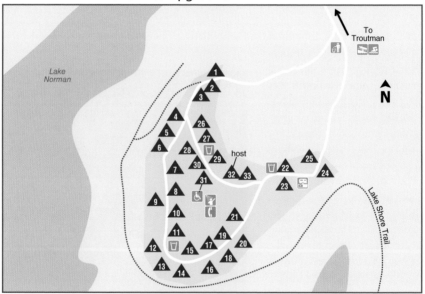

GETTING THERE

From Exit 42 on I-77, just south of Statesville, North Carolina, turn left to head north on US 21, and go 2.7 miles to the town of Troutman. Take a sharp left on Wagner Street, which becomes Perth Road, and follow it 1.5 miles. Turn right on State Park Road, and follow it 2 miles to enter the park. Continue another 3.3 miles to the campground. The park's address is 759 State Park Road, Troutman, NC 28166.

GPS COORDINATES: N35° 38.812'   W80° 56.526'

23

Morrow Mountain State Park Campground

Beauty ★★★★ Privacy ★★★ Spaciousness ★★★★ Quiet ★★★★ Security ★★★★★ Cleanliness ★★★★

This mountainous getaway on the Piedmont features hiking, boating, fishing, and swimming.

The peaks of Morrow Mountain will surprise you. They aren't the "big highs" of western North Carolina, but if you want a touch and feel of the mountains without having to make the trip west, come here. Relative to the terrain of the surrounding Piedmont, the Uwharrie Mountains rise to offer vertical relief and a mountain aura to the upper Pee Dee River Valley. Back in the 1930s, local residents noted the area's beauty and strove to develop a park. Today the 4,700-acre park offers a large campground, more than 30 miles of trails, and water recreation on Lake Tillery, which is located at the base of the mountains.

Normally a campground with more than 100 sites can resemble a mini–tent city. Morrow Mountain, however, bucks the trend. Three separate loops are spread over a wide area, each with its own bathhouse, giving the impression of three individual campgrounds rather than one oversize tent dealership. Loop A houses campsites 1–36 on a slight slope. A mix of pines, sweet gum, cedar, and understory trees such as dogwood shades the camps.

Loop B, featuring woodsy sites 37–68, is the most isolated and the most popular. It is located on a spur ridge with land dropping off on the outside of the loop, creating a mountain atmosphere. Where the slope is excessive, the sites have been leveled. Try to get one of the sites on the outside of the loop, as these offer more space. Also, the sites are a bit closer together than those on Loop A. Some have parking spurs that pull directly to the sites, while others necessitate a short walk to the camping area. The end of the loop backs against a narrow hollow, creating additional sloping.

A young girl looks out on Lake Tillery.

courtesy of North Carolina Division of Parks and Recreation

KEY INFORMATION

CONTACT: 704-982-4402; ncparks.gov
/morrow-mountain-state-park

OPEN: Year-round (only Camping Area C
open in winter)

SITES: 105, 6 cabins

EACH SITE HAS: Tent pad, picnic table, fire
grate, lantern post; 22 have electricity

WHEELCHAIR ACCESS: Yes

ASSIGNMENT: First come, first served and by
reservation (877-722-6762; ncparks.gov
/make-reservation)

REGISTRATION: Ranger will come by to
register you

AMENITIES: Hot showers, flush toilets,
water spigots

PARKING: At campsites only; must be on
designated parking pad

FEE: $15–$17; $18–$22 electric, depending
on season

ELEVATION: 450'

RESTRICTIONS:

PETS: On leash only

FIRES: In fire rings only

ALCOHOL: Prohibited

OTHER: 6 people and 2 tents/site; 14-day
stay limit in a 30-day period; gates closed
7–10 p.m. (depending on season) to 7 a.m.

Loop C was my choice, with sites 69–106. This loop is the most level, has sites that are more widespread than those in Loops A and B, and is the only loop open in winter. This loop is bisected by a crossroad. Some sites along it are open and grassy—perfect in colder months—while pines shade others. Younger hardwoods shade yet other sites. A campground host is here for your safety and convenience, except in winter. Morrow Mountain fills on holiday weekends and a few ideal-weather weekends during spring and fall. Reservations eliminate any campsite availability concerns.

When asked why campers come here, one park ranger summed it up in one word: variety. The park offers both waterfront and mountaintop attractions. Lake Tillery, a 17-mile impoundment of the upper Pee Dee River, offers the water recreation. Campers with boats can use the park ramp to ply the lake, fishing for striped bass, largemouth bass, crappie, bream, and catfish. If you don't have a boat, you can rent a canoe or a sit-on-top kayak for exploring the lake. Otherwise, use the 120-foot fishing pier. The park also has the only swimming pool in the North Carolina state park system. Open during the summer, it features a bathhouse constructed of native stone in the 1930s.

The park's trail system stretches from one end of its boundaries to the other. Half the trails are hiker only, while the other half are hiker-and-horse paths. The Rocks Trail leads directly from the campground to an outcrop overlooking Lake Tillery. The Hattaway Mountain Trail is less used and more challenging, offering winter vistas. Take the Sugarloaf Mountain Trail and the Morrow Mountain Trail for far-reaching views of the lake and land beyond. Of course, a road leads to instant vistas atop Morrow Mountain. Speaking of roads, bicyclers like to pedal their way around the park; be advised, though, that some of these roads are steep.

Visitors should explore the park's history too. The Kron House re-creates the home of the area's first doctor, Francis Kron. The home, office, infirmary, and greenhouse appear much as they did in the 1870s. Weekend interpretive programs tell of the events of Kron's day and other aspects of the state park. You ought to take the good doctor's advice and settle down here for a spell. Oh, and bring your tent.

Morrow Mountain State Park Overview

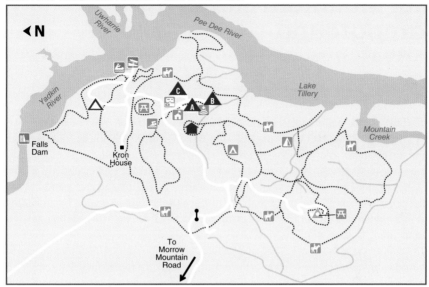

Morrow Mountain State Park Campgrounds and Cabins

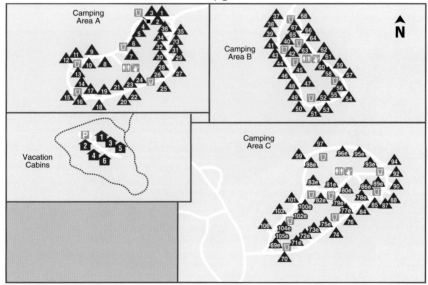

GETTING THERE

From the intersection of NC 740 and NC 1549 in Badin, North Carolina, head southeast on NC 740, and go 4.8 miles. Make a sharp left on Morrow Mountain Road, and go 4 miles. Keep left to stay on Morrow Mountain Road, and go 1.3 miles to reach the campground. The park's address is 49104 Morrow Mountain Road, Albemarle, NC 28001.

GPS COORDINATES: N35° 22.298'   W80° 04.107'

24

Pilot Mountain State Park Campground

Beauty ★★★★ Privacy ★★★ Spaciousness ★★ Quiet ★★★★ Security ★★★★★ Cleanliness ★★★

Pilot Mountain is a North Carolina landmark.

North Carolina has many special mountains, but when it comes to memorable and distinct landmarks, Pilot Mountain takes the cake. On the edge of the Piedmont, the mountain—named for its status as a way marker for all who passed through the area—rises from the surrounding lands to climax in a circular peak of nearly vertical rock walls with a wooded cap. The park is now a great destination for tent campers. Hiking and rock climbing are the primary pastimes here. The mountain area of the park is complemented by an additional segment on the Yadkin River that has a living history farm, fishing and paddling opportunities, and hiking trails.

The campground is situated, not surprisingly, on a slope of Pilot Mountain. Before you imagine having to buckle yourself in to keep from rolling off a hill, realize that the sites have been leveled, for the most part, and all sites have level tent pads, making mountainside slumber more likely.

A hiking trail runs alongside the crags of Pilot Mountain.

KEY INFORMATION

CONTACT: 336-325-2355; ncparks.gov
/pilot-mountain-state-park

OPEN: Mid-March–November

SITES: 48

EACH SITE HAS: Tent pad, picnic table,
fire ring

WHEELCHAIR ACCESS: Yes

ASSIGNMENT: First come, first served and by
reservation (877-722-6762; ncparks.gov
/make-reservation)

REGISTRATION: Ranger will come by to
register you

AMENITIES: Hot showers, flush toilets,
water spigots

PARKING: At campsites only

FEE: $10–$23

ELEVATION: 1,000'

RESTRICTIONS:

PETS: On 6' leash or shorter only

FIRES: In fire rings only

ALCOHOL: Prohibited

OTHER: 6 people/site; 32' trailer-length limit;
gathering firewood in the park is not
allowed; gates closed 8–10 p.m. (depending
on season) to 7 a.m.; fireworks prohibited

The paved campground loop has paved parking spurs to minimize erosion and keep your car from sliding off the mountain. Overhead, chestnut oaks, dogwoods, and hickories shade the campsites. Mountain laurels and young trees make a passable understory. Many of the sites are separated from the parking spur, necessitating a short walk into the woods and some-times up or down steps. This short walk actually increases campsite privacy, but squeezing in sites where the terrain allows compromises their size. Most sites are average in size, while others are small. Limiting your gear will increase your site choices. Cruise around the loop, passing the Grindstone Trail beyond site 16. A modern bathhouse stands near site 25. From here, the loop circles downhill. Sometimes, a site's picnic table and tent pad are spaced a bit apart because of the terrain. However, the sloping mountainside enhances the camping atmo-sphere here on Pilot Mountain, where 95% of the sites are desirable.

Weekdays are very quiet, and, surprisingly, Pilot Mountain fills only on holiday week-ends. Any other time you should be able to get a site. You will be sharing the campground with young couples, families, the occasional rock climber, and other folks who come here to get a firsthand look at the unusual mountain.

The view looking up at Pilot Mountain as you arrive arouses a curiosity to see what it's like looking down on the surrounding landscape. Here are the statistics: Pilot Mountain stands 2,421 feet high, more than 1,400 feet above the surrounding countryside. On a clear day, you can see more than 3,000 square miles from Little Pinnacle Overlook.

More than 27 miles of trails course through the park's mountain and river sections. Take the Ledge Spring Trail for a trip along sheer rock bluffs. The Jomeokee Trail circles the crest of the circular mountain. The Grindstone Trail leads from the campground and allows access to the other high-country paths. The longest trail is the Corridor Trail, which con-nects the river and mountain sections of the park. The river section of the park is centered on the Yadkin Islands, on the Yadkin River. The Horne Creek Trail starts near the Horne Creek Living Historical Farm where, on weekends, folks dressed in early-20th-century period clothes go about the business of farm life from that era. Check ahead with the park to make sure a demonstration is going on during your visit. The nearby Yadkin River offers

165 miles of canoeing and kayaking possibilities. The Shoals Access site is just upstream of the Yadkin Islands. Your river experience should contrast well with your more-solid explorations from atop Pilot Mountain.

Pilot Mountain State Park Campground

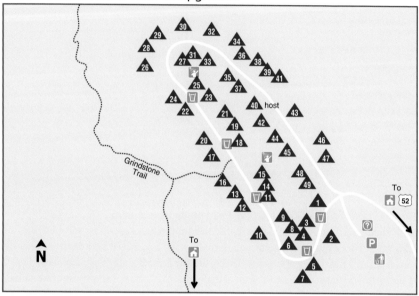

GETTING THERE

From Winston-Salem, North Carolina, take I-40 to Exit 193B and merge onto US 52 N. Go 24.3 miles, and take Exit 131 for Pilot Mountain State Park. Turn left on Pilot Knob Park Road, and go 0.3 mile. Turn left to stay on Pilot Knob Park Road, and follow it 1.5 miles to the campground. The park's address is 1792 Pilot Knob Park Road, Pinnacle, NC 27699.

GPS COORDINATES: N36° 20.622'   W80° 28.837'

NORTH CAROLINA COAST & COASTAL PLAIN

The lighthouse on Ocracoke Island *(see campground 33, page 110)*

25

Carolina Beach State Park Campground

Beauty ★★★★ Privacy ★★★ Spaciousness ★★★★ Quiet ★★★ Security ★★★★★ Cleanliness ★★★

Many attractions are within a short drive of this lesser-used oceanside campground.

This area of the Carolinas certainly has some amazing natural attributes, but the most unusual of all may be the Venus flytrap. Perhaps you have heard of it. The modified leaves of this plant close rapidly when an insect touches tiny hairs on the leaves' insides, trapping the insect, which then becomes dinner. The Venus flytrap grows only on land located within a 60-mile radius of Wilmington, North Carolina. Carolina Beach State Park has a trail where you can see this unusual plant. The park also has a fine, lesser-used campgrounds as well as many attractions within a 10-mile radius of the campground, such as beaches, historic sites, and even an aquarium.

With all there is to do here, you should find the campground very appealing as a base camp. It is located in piney woods near Snow's Cut, a waterway connecting the wide Cape Fear River to the Intracoastal Waterway. Pine trees tower over the two campground loops. Live oaks, water oaks, and other hardwoods are mixed in with the pines. Clumpy brush

The waterside trail entices visitors.

courtesy of North Carolina Division of Parks and Recreation

KEY INFORMATION

CONTACT: 910-458-8206; ncparks.gov
/carolina-beach-state-park

OPEN: Year-round

SITES: 79, 4 cabins

EACH SITE HAS: Picnic table, fire ring;
9 have electricity

WHEELCHAIR ACCESS: Yes

ASSIGNMENT: First come, first served and by
reservation (877-722-6762; ncparks.gov
/make-reservation)

REGISTRATION: At park store and marina

AMENITIES: Hot showers, flush toilets,
water spigots

PARKING: At campsites only; 2 vehicles/site

FEE: $15–$23; $18–$28 electric

ELEVATION: 10'

RESTRICTIONS:

PETS: On leash only

FIRES: In fire rings only

ALCOHOL: Prohibited

OTHER: 6 people/site; gates closed 6–
10 p.m. (depending on season) to 7 a.m.

---

grows here and there among the woods, adding privacy. A drive on the paved campground road through the first loop reveals large sites with sand-and-pine-needle floors. Nine of the first 15 campsites offer electricity. The Snow's Cut Trail leads toward a maritime forest near campsite 21. I enjoyed site 25, where the filtering sunlight helped dry my gear after a storm pushed through the previous night. A bathhouse centers the loop.

A short road with large campsites along it leads to the second loop, which hosts sites 48–82 and opens only when the first loop fills. The sites look little used in this loop, but the first loop doesn't get a whole lot of business either. The second loop, from which the Sugarloaf Trail leaves at site 54, also has large camps and a bathhouse in the center.

The campground fills most weekends from Memorial Day through Fourth of July weekend. After that, the heat keeps most campers away until fall, when cooler-weather weekends become busy but usually do not see the campground full. A campsite can be had most spring weekends and anytime during winter. We came during fall—the weather was ideal, and the insects weren't bothersome.

There are plenty of beach accesses near Carolina Beach State Park on nearby Pleasure Island. I recommend driving 5 miles to Fort Fisher State Recreation Area. It features 7 miles of state-owned beach with summer lifeguards in the designated ocean-swimming area. Four-wheel-drive vehicles can access other areas along the beach. The recreation area is popular with beachcombers. The North Carolina Aquarium at Fort Fisher is a great place to check out marine life up close, and Fort Fisher State Historic Site, where you can learn about the history of this Confederate Civil War bunker, is located nearby. Many folks like to tour the USS *North Carolina* battleship, conspicuously located in the Cape Fear River near Wilmington.

Don't forget, though, about all the fun stuff to do at Carolina Beach State Park. The area is laced with hiking trails that crisscross numerous natural communities. The Flytrap Trail features the famous Venus flytrap. The Sugarloaf Trail passes through tidal flats and pinewoods. Snow's Cut Trail leads to the Intracoastal Waterway. The 6-plus miles of trails are hiked mostly during cooler months.

For anglers, a fishing deck leading into the Cape Fear River is near the park marina. This location attracts anglers going for croaker, flounder, and striped bass, in all types of weather.

The marina sells plenty of bait and tackle, and campers with boats will enjoy the convenience of the boat launch. Furthermore, during the warm seasons, a local concessionaire offers kayak and paddleboard rentals, as well as guided paddling tours.

With an abundance of recreational and sightseeing opportunities close by, camping at Carolina Beach is pleasurable as well as convenient.

Carolina Beach State Park Campground

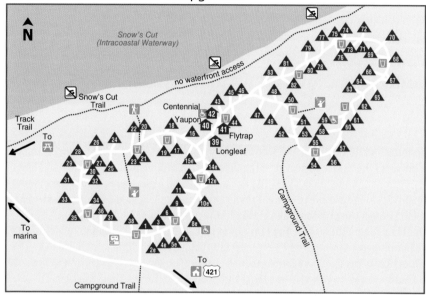

GETTING THERE

From the intersection of US 17 and US 421 in Wilmington, North Carolina, drive south on US 421 for 0.9 mile, and turn left to remain on US 421. Go 5.7 miles, and turn right to stay on US 421 S. In 6.6 miles, after crossing the Intracoastal Waterway, turn right on Dow Road, reaching the park in 0.3 mile on your right. Turn right on State Park Road, and go 0.5 mile to the campground. The park's address is 1010 State Park Road, Carolina Beach, NC 28428.

GPS COORDINATES: N34° 02.983'   W77° 54.465'

26

Cliffs of the Neuse State Park Campground

Beauty ★★★ Privacy ★★★ Spaciousness ★★★★ Quiet ★★★★ Security ★★★★★ Cleanliness ★★★

This underutilized campground stands next to some surprising terrain on the coastal plain.

Often state parks are established to protect a natural resource unique to the state. Cliffs of the Neuse fits this mold. Hills are limited here on the coastal plain, and cliffs are rare. Interesting geologic events occurred to form the cliffs along the Neuse River. In 1944 local landowner Lionel Weil proposed that this unusual area, which also harbors a mixture of plants representing different areas of the state, be preserved as a state park. Private individuals banded together to donate the land for the park to the state of North Carolina. More property was added later and an infrastructure built to complement the cliffs, including a lake, trails, and an uncrowded campground that is a great weekend retreat.

The campground lies beneath rich woodland on slightly sloping land. Tall pines mix with a variety of hardwoods, including hickory, beech, and water oak. The brushy understory of

Fishing the Neuse River

courtesy of North Carolina Division of Parks and Recreation

KEY INFORMATION

CONTACT: 919-778-6234; ncparks.gov
/cliffs-of-the-neuse-state-park

OPEN: Year-round

SITES: 35

EACH SITE HAS: Picnic table, fire grate;
12 have electricity and water

WHEELCHAIR ACCESS: Yes

ASSIGNMENT: First come, first served and by
reservation (877-722-6762; ncparks.gov
/make-reservation)

REGISTRATION: Ranger will come by to
register you

AMENITIES: Hot showers, flush toilets,
water spigots

PARKING: At campsites only; 2 vehicles/site

FEE: $15–$23; $23–$33 electric

ELEVATION: 125'

RESTRICTIONS:

PETS: On leash only

FIRES: In fire rings only

ALCOHOL: Prohibited

OTHER: 6 people and 2 tents/site; gates
closed 6–9 p.m. (depending on season)
to 7 a.m.

holly, young sweet gum, and other small trees can be thick in one spot and open in another, creating privacy at one campsite and openness at the next. The first few sites are wooded around the edges and open in the center. Pine needles and sand carpet the sites. I enjoyed site 12 because it shaded a strong September sun. Luckily, a cool night followed. Barefoot campers should avoid site 14, as a holly tree stands in its center.

The loop curves around and reaches an area with limited shade starting at campsite 20. Thick brush shields the sites on their sides, but they are open overhead. Lush grass carpets these sites, which show less use than the shaded ones. Thick woods resume past site 25. The loop curves uphill, making the last few sites a bit too sloped for good camping. Sites 1–6, 8, 10, 12, 26, 28, and 30 have been electrified. Interestingly, small cabins have been placed on sites 7, 9, and 11.

Overall, the sites are large and desirable for tent campers, making the light use of this campground surprising. It only fills on holiday weekends, so Cliffs of the Neuse is great for avoiding the crowds at other times, especially during spring and fall. Ideal-weather weekends during these seasons only fill half the 35 sites.

Water spigots are laid out at convenient intervals along the loop; the bathhouse is accessed by trails spoking into the loop's center. For your safety, the park gates are locked every night. If an emergency occurs, use the gate code given to campers.

An emergency may be the only time you have to get in your car while at the park. Access to all facilities is just a walk away. For example, a trail leads from the campground to the park museum. Here, the formation of the Cliffs of the Neuse is explained in a manner that even the geologically challenged like me can understand; park history is detailed as well. The actual Cliffs of the Neuse stand just feet from the museum. Walk along the split rail fence to garner some views that are unusual for this region, while the Neuse River beckons below. Take the 350 Yard Trail along the cliff to the river's edge. Here, anglers may be lazing away the day, going for largemouth bass but more likely catching bream and bluegill. The trail bridges gurgling Mill Creek, where a facility for grinding corn once stood. The Galax Trail starts across the water. Here lies an isolated pocket of the galax plant, normally a mountain species of ground cover. The Bird Trail loops along the Neuse River, providing more bank-fishing opportunities there, as well as along Still Creek, where whiskey was once made. These trails are great for families with kids or folks who just want a light leg-stretcher.

Seeing the Neuse River made me want to go on a float trip. The most popular run is from the NC 111 bridge down to the hamlet of Seven Springs, a distance of 8 miles. Park rangers occasionally lead trips down this stretch of river.

The state park offers water recreation of its own. The upper reaches of Mill Creek have been dammed, forming a spring-fed, 11-acre lake. There is an elaborate swim area, with a wide swim beach adjacent to a large, grassy lawn. It is open Memorial Day–Labor Day. A changing building and snack bar are also located here. Rental boats are available from the park to ply the lake. However, private boats are not allowed. As you have read, the unique features that are the Cliffs of the Neuse have been protected and enhanced by this state park. Now come check them out for yourself.

Cliffs of the Neuse State Park Campground

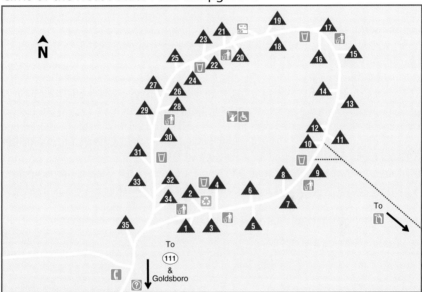

GETTING THERE

Take I-795 S to Exit 25B in Goldsboro, North Carolina. Head east on US 70, and go 0.6 mile. Use the right lane to merge onto US 117 N/US 70 E, and go 7 miles. Turn right on NC 111, and follow it 8.4 miles. Turn left on Park Entrance Road, and follow it 0.7 mile to the campground. The park's address is 240 Park Entrance Road, Seven Springs, NC 28578.

GPS COORDINATES: N35° 14.315' W77° 53.297'

27

⛺ Frisco Campground

Beauty ★★★★★ Privacy ★ Spaciousness ★★ Quiet ★★★★ Security ★★★★★ Cleanliness ★★

Pitch your tent among the rolling dunes of Cape Hatteras National Seashore.

Frisco Campground offers some phenomenal oceanside scenery. Located in the Cape Hatteras National Seashore, the campground is situated among dunes so hilly that you might think you were in the mountains instead of at the beach. OK, that's an exaggeration, but oceanside topography doesn't get much more vertical than this in the Tar Heel State. Beach activities such as surf fishing, beachcombing, kayaking, and visiting lighthouses are on the agenda. Or maybe the agenda is to just sit by the Atlantic Ocean and listen to the waves roll in.

But make no mistake—this oceanside environment is harsh and unforgiving. This is what accounts for the stark beauty of the Outer Banks: a relentless ocean pounding against the sand, rolling dunes where sea oats cling to life, wind-sculpted trees growing in dune swales, a strong sun beating down on the very openness that is the banks. The campground reflects this stark beauty. The sites are appealing, but they are exposed to wind, sun, and mosquitoes.

The campground is laid out in a big loop with six roads crossing it. The loop overlays a series of dunes that are ever increasing in height as you head away from the ocean, which runs parallel to the campground and is about 150 yards distant. Scattered cedars, oaks, and pines grow mostly brushy, looking nothing like they would on the mainland. The wind keeps these trees from growing straight and tall. They are most stunted on the tops of the dunes, if they grow there at all. In the swales, where the wind is not as strong, the trees more resemble their inland cousins, but trees that grow over a person's head are few.

Sea oats wave in the foreground; the Cape Hatteras Lighthouse can be seen beyond them.

KEY INFORMATION

CONTACT: Cape Hatteras National Seashore, 252-473-2111; nps.gov/caha

OPEN: April–late November

SITES: 120, 7 RV sites

EACH SITE HAS: Picnic table, upright grill

WHEELCHAIR ACCESS: Yes

ASSIGNMENT: First come, first served and by reservation (877-444-6777; recreation.gov)

REGISTRATION: At campground entrance booth

AMENITIES: Cold showers, water spigots, flush toilets

PARKING: At campsites only; 2 vehicles/site; must be parked on paved surface

FEE: $28

ELEVATION: 50'

RESTRICTIONS:

PETS: On leash only

FIRES: In upright grills only, below high tide line on beach

ALCOHOL: At campsites only

OTHER: 6 people/site; 14-day stay limit in a 30-day period Memorial Day–Labor Day

Nevertheless, campsites with even a modicum of shade will be snapped up. Most sites are completely in the open, cutting privacy to a minimum.

As the main loop curves around, pass some pine trees in the low area between the campground and the beach, which is accessed by two boardwalks. The road rises remarkably high, maybe a couple hundred feet. The sites on the back of the loop begin to overlook the ocean, offering stunning panoramas. Just like any sites here, these have their pluses and minuses. The open sites will have the wind, which cuts down on mosquitoes, but if the wind is cold, then the openness is a negative. If the sun is blaring down, as it often is, then the lack of shade can be a problem. Bringing a screen shelter can eliminate both sun and bug problems. Many sites are small, so you will have to be flexible in how you set up camp. I stayed in site P-56 and enjoyed the afternoon shade, but the mosquitoes were a bit troublesome.

Campers usually end up finding a site to suit them (do some driving around once you get here). No matter your location, a bathhouse and water spigot are close by. Frisco fills on major holidays and a few other perfect-weather weekends in summer. Otherwise, you should be able to get a site. Reservations can quash any availability worries.

Four-wheel-drive vehicles can access the beach at many areas of Cape Hatteras National Seashore. These access points are referred to as ramps, one of which is adjacent to the campground. Most campers just use the boardwalks to reach the beach by foot. In either case, you have miles of shoreline to enjoy, whether you are surf casting or surfing with a board. A fishing pier is just west of the campground, as is a designated swim beach with a bathhouse.

Cape Hatteras Lighthouse is just a short drive away. It made the news two decades ago when it was moved to keep it from falling into the shifting sea. You can climb the lighthouse and get a grand view, or you can walk the nearby Buxton Woods Trail, operated in conjunction with the Nature Conservancy. Supplies are available in the village of Frisco, which is conveniently just a mile from the campground. And after staying a night or two, a mile may be all you will want to get away from here.

Frisco Campground

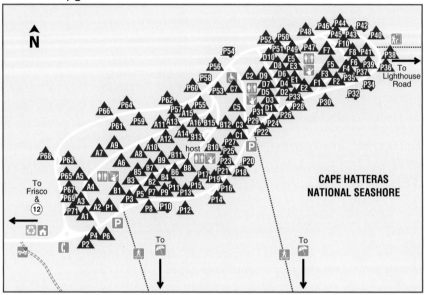

GETTING THERE

From the intersection of US 64 and US 158 just south of Nags Head, North Carolina, drive south on NC 12 for 53.5 miles to the hamlet of Frisco. Turn left on Billy Mitchell Road, and follow it 1.1 miles to reach the campground. The campground's address is 53415 Billy Mitchell Road, Frisco, NC 27936.

GPS COORDINATES: N35° 14.085′   W75° 36.436′

28

Goose Creek State Park Campground

Beauty ★★★★ Privacy ★★★★★ Spaciousness ★★★★★ Quiet ★★★★★ Security ★★★★★
Cleanliness ★★★★★

Enjoy some of the coastal plain's finest wetlands at this quiet state park.

This state park features an informative environmental-education center presenting first-rate displays and information about North Carolina's wetlands, where the interplay between land, river, and ocean forms a rich ecosystem that is explained for all to understand. The center is worth a stop, but an even better idea is to explore this state park's ecosystem for yourself. Gain firsthand knowledge about the preserve on the edge of the Pamlico River via foot and paddling trails, or launch your activities from the park campground, which could hardly get better from this tent camper's point of view.

The so-called primitive campground is set on a piece of high ground between Flatty and Goose Creeks. A narrow road stretches out beneath tall loblolly pines, complemented by hickory, oak, holly, and bay trees. The forest understory is light. Be careful driving the

campground road, as trees grow so close alongside it that you might nick one with your vehicle. A sign at the beginning of the campground states NO LARGE RVS. Soon come to campsite 1. A gravel parking spur leads to a large site shaded by pines, oaks, and hollies. Site 1 was so alluring that I claimed it immediately without looking at the rest of the campground, but it's far from the only good site here. Site 2 is a good 75 yards down the road—the sites here are as widespread as you are going to get—and has a gravel parking pad with a short walkway leading to the site. (Most sites here require a short walk to reach the actual camping areas.) Past one of four water spigots, site 3 is a double, 200 feet from the road. Site 4 is a drive-up site. Across from site 4 is one of two

The boardwalk protects the boggy pathway.

courtesy of North Carolina Division of Parks and Recreation

KEY INFORMATION

CONTACT: 252-923-0052; ncparks.gov /goose-creek-state-park

OPEN: Year-round

SITES: 14

EACH SITE HAS: Picnic table, fire ring, lantern post

WHEELCHAIR ACCESS: Yes

ASSIGNMENT: First come, first served and by reservation (877-722-6762; ncparks.gov /make-reservation)

REGISTRATION: Ranger will come by to register you

AMENITIES: Water spigot, vault toilet

PARKING: At campsites only

FEE: $10

ELEVATION: 10'

RESTRICTIONS:

PETS: On leash only

FIRES: In fire rings only

ALCOHOL: Prohibited

OTHER: 6 people/site; gates closed 6–9 p.m. (depending on season) to 8 a.m.

---

composting toilets using the latest ventilation technology, which does make a difference in the odor department.

Keep going down the road. Site 5 is also a drive-up site and has an upright grill in addition to a fire ring. Site 6 is a walk-in site in a shady flat. (All the sites here are level, by the way, and designated parking spots are provided for each walk-in site.) Site 7 is on the right, across the road from Flatty Creek Trail. Site 8 is a walk-in site scattered with pines. Site 9 is another walk-in site. Site 10 has many hardwoods shading it. The last four sites, 11–14, require a longer walk but are also closest to Goose Creek. Site 12 looks toward water on three sides, though the water is a good 100 feet away. Campsites 13 and 14 also have aquatic views. An auto turnaround is at the end of the road, along with an observation deck that stretches into Goose Creek.

Spring and fall are the best times to camp at Goose Creek. The campground fills a couple of great-weather weekends per season. A site will be available any time of the year during the week, although summer is too hot and buggy.

Now, explore the wetlands that make Goose Creek so special. You may want to visit the environmental education center first to gain an understanding of the ecosystem and to learn what to look for, then take off. The Palmetto Boardwalk behind the nature center offers interpretive signage showing you the wetlands firsthand. Campers can use the small, sandy shore at the campground's edge to launch their canoes or kayaks into the water. Here, you can join Goose Creek and head upstream, exploring not only the natural history of the area but also the human history. Check out relics of an old logging operation in addition to wildflowers and wildlife, especially birds. Flatty and Mallard Creeks are also good paddling destinations, as is the shoreline along Pamlico River. The brackish river supports both saltwater and freshwater species, so bring your pole and angle for flounder, bream, black drum, and largemouth bass. A swim beach, which requires a short walk, is on the Pamlico too.

Landlubbers have choices as well. Ivey Gut Trail leaves from the upper end of the campground and curves alongside Goose Creek for a 2-mile, one-way trek. Flatty Creek Trail is also accessible directly from the campground. It makes a 1-mile loop through the woods and across boardwalks to reach an observation deck along Flatty Creek. Goose Creek Trail is the park's longest, at 2.9 miles. Here, you can enjoy some of the park's three types of primary wetlands—hardwood swamp, cypress gum swamp, and brackish marsh. Ragged Point Trail leads to a boardwalk and observation deck. Live Oak Trail travels beneath stately trees draped with Spanish moss. Exploring this park is a joy you can experience many times over, especially with such a nice campground.

Goose Creek State Park Campground

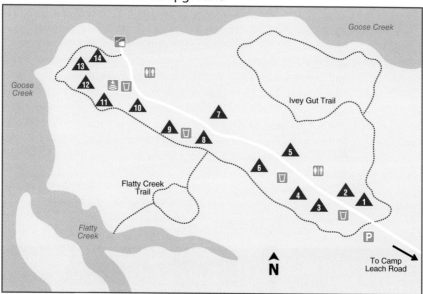

GETTING THERE

From I-95, take Exit 119A to merge onto US 264 E. Go 4 miles, and continue straight on US 264 E for another 32.7 miles. Take Exit 73B to remain on US 264 E, and go 9.8 miles to Greenville. Turn left to stay on US 264 E, and go 26.5 miles. Turn right on Camp Leach Road/NC 1334, and follow it 2.2 miles to the park on your right. Go 1.5 miles, keeping right, to reach the campground. The park's address is 2190 Camp Leach Road, Washington, NC 27889.

GPS COORDINATES: N35° 28.356'   W76° 55.325'

29

Jones Lake State Park Campground

Beauty ★★★★ Privacy ★★★ Spaciousness ★★★★ Quiet ★★★★ Security ★★★★★ Cleanliness ★★★★

Pitch your tent among the longleaf pines by this Carolina bay lake.

Have you ever heard of bay lakes? These natural wonders stretch from Florida to New Jersey but are most prominent in the Carolinas. They are usually oval shaped, pointed on a northwest-to-southeast axis, and no deeper than 10 feet. Theories about the origins of these lakes range from meteors crashing into Earth to gigantic prehistoric whales carving holes in ancient shallow seas with their tails. *Bay* refers to the preponderance of sweet bay and red bay trees growing around them. A bay lake called Jones Lake is the centerpiece of this quiet state park with a good campground that is simply not used as much as it deserves.

The campground and recreation areas of Jones Lake State Park are on the southeastern shore of the 224-acre lake, which is ringed by cypress, bay, titi, and other moisture-tolerant flora. The campground is situated in slightly higher, sandier terrain. Here, longleaf pine and turkey oaks predominate. These two trees are part of the longleaf–wire grass ecosystem, which once covered more than 20 million acres in the Southeast. This open woodland makes for a very attractive campground setting.

A paved road loops around the campground. The large campsites have floors of sand and pine needles. Pond and loblolly pines also grow among the longleafs. Turkey oaks,

Ecosystem recovery after a prescribed burn

courtesy of North Carolina Division of Parks and Recreation

KEY INFORMATION

CONTACT: 910-588-4550; ncparks.gov
/jones-lake-state-park

OPEN: Year-round

SITES: 19, 1 RV site

EACH SITE HAS: Picnic table, fire grate;
site 3 has electricity and water

WHEELCHAIR ACCESS: Yes

ASSIGNMENT: First come, first served and by
reservation (877-722-6762; ncparks.gov
/make-reservation)

REGISTRATION: Ranger will come by to
register you

AMENITIES: Hot showers, water spigots,
flush toilets

PARKING: At campsites only

FEE: $15–$23; $18–$28 electric

ELEVATION: 75'

RESTRICTIONS:

PETS: On leash only

FIRES: In fire rings only

ALCOHOL: Prohibited

OTHER: 6 people/site; gates closed 6–9 p.m.
(depending on season) to 8 a.m.

with their short limbs and scrubby appearance, stand beneath the pines. Young bay trees, sassafras, and cane shoot from the ground. The sites have a mixture of sun and shade but are more open than not. At virtually any other campground, privacy might be compromised, but this attractive destination's surprising unpopularity will likely leave you with no neighbors around.

Beyond campsite 7, a path leads from the campground to the Lake Trail and a fishing pier. The vegetation thickens as a wetland backs the sites. Pass the access road to reach the group campground and sites that are more open, though most have enough shade to make it through a hot day. One site at the park has water and electricity.

A bathhouse stands in the center of the loop. Summer and early fall will find younger families from nearby military bases pitching a tent. Campers can count on getting sites just about any weekend, except for summer-holiday weekends. Even then, though, your chances of getting a site are pretty good.

A visitor center stands near Jones Lake and is the center of activity. Interpretive ranger programs are held on weekends. A pretty picnic area, dotted with scattered trees among lush grass, overlooks the lake, and a dock leads out to a boathouse where canoes and paddleboats can be rented at very reasonable rates. The park swim beach is here, too, marked by buoys that extend far out into the dark waters.

If you want to hike, take the Bay Trail. It extends 4 miles, encircling the scenic body of water. Short side trails lead to the lake's edge and afford good views. Beginning near the nature center, you can take a shorter walk on the Cedar Loop Trail, which makes a 1-mile loop.

A boat launch enables those with their own watercraft to access the lake; motors of 10 horsepower and below are allowed. Canoes and paddleboats may be rented if you are without. Jones Lake is highly acidic, which limits fishing. However, you can vie for yellow perch, pickerel, catfish, and small sunfish. A fishing pier extends into the lake from near the campground. Nearby Salters Lake, also a Carolina bay lake within the park's 2,000-plus acres, is managed as a natural area. Visitors can access it after getting a permit from the ranger station. Carved from the surrounding Bladen Lakes State Forest, Jones Lake State Park is quiet and undeveloped, which, as a tent camper, you will enjoy.

Jones Lake State Park Campground

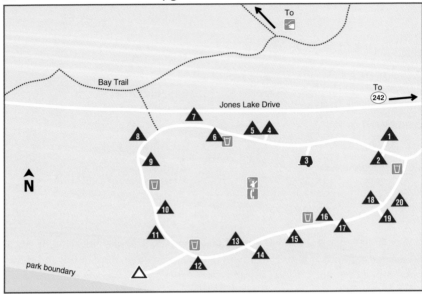

GETTING THERE

From I-95, take Exit 49, and head east on NC 210/NC 53. In 7.3 miles keep straight on Turnbull Road (the road becomes Old Fayetteville Road), and go 13.5 miles. Turn right on NC 242, and drive 9.2 miles to the state park, which will be on your right. The park's address is 4117 NC 242, North Elizabethtown, NC 28337.

GPS COORDINATES: N34° 40.772'   W78° 35.858'

30

Lumber River State Park:

PRINCESS ANN ACCESS CAMPGROUND

Beauty ★★★★ Privacy ★★★★ Spaciousness ★★★ Quiet ★★★★ Security ★★★★★ Cleanliness ★★★★

All the camps on the Wild and Scenic Lumber River are walk-in tent sites.

As a federally designated Wild and Scenic River, the Lumber is officially special. The state of North Carolina recognized the river's beauty and added a serpentine state park along it, protecting wild stretches and developing other park units that allow access to riverside camping, as well as water-access points with restrooms and picnic areas. This Princess Ann unit of the park has a walk-in tent campground where you can enjoy the river and the land around it. Nearby outfitters allow even the boatless to float down the Lumber and return to this campground, which seems to have tent campers in mind.

The campground at Princess Ann unit is located in lush, dark, and cool woods near the Princess Ann access boat ramp (the Chalk Bank unit of Lumber River State Park, 50 miles distant, has 14 campsites and is also a worthy destination). Back at Princess Ann, seven campsites are grouped together, two of which are directly along the river. The main camping area is set in luxuriant woods on a sloping hill leading toward the Lumber. Water oaks, sweet gums, and understory oaks dominate the forest; smaller bay trees have to work hard

Princess Ann Landing

courtesy of North Carolina Division of Parks and Recreation

KEY INFORMATION

CONTACT: 910-628-9844; ncparks.gov
/lumber-river-state-park

OPEN: Year-round

SITES: 9

EACH SITE HAS: Tent pad, picnic table,
fire ring, lantern post

WHEELCHAIR ACCESS: Yes

ASSIGNMENT: First come, first served and by
reservation (877-722-6762; ncparks.gov
/make-reservation)

REGISTRATION: Online, by phone, or ranger
will come by to register you

AMENITIES: Water spigot, vault toilet

PARKING: At boat-ramp parking area

FEE: $10

ELEVATION: 80'

RESTRICTIONS:
PETS: On leash only

FIRES: In fire rings only

ALCOHOL: Prohibited

OTHER: 6 people/site; 14-day stay limit in
a 30-day period; gates closed 7–10 p.m.
(depending on season) to 7 a.m.; permit
required

to gain light from the thick overhead canopy. A paved path leads to disabled-access camp-site 1. This site, like all the others, has been leveled using landscaping timbers. A gravel path continues to site 2. Site 3 is at the lower end of the hill, closer to the river. Site 4 has oaks with outstretched limbs shading it. Site 5 is closer to the river. Site 6 has the farthest walk, but even this is no more than 75 yards. This site is open in the center and has the most pri-vacy of the sites around it. Site 7 is highest on the hill. It is very shady and has pine needles for a carpet, but it's small and was added as an afterthought. A short trail leads to the final two campsites. Walk past the boat ramp and begin heading downstream along the beautiful Lumber. Reach site 8 first, then site 9. Cypress trees draped in Spanish moss stand along the river. A cypress-gum swamp lies on the other side of the campsites. This area is level and shady, exuding the beauty of the river.

Bald cypresses, with their knees protruding from the water, line the river, and rich stands of cane overlook the tannin-stained, tea-colored water. A bluff that rises from this side of the river attracted early settlers who formed the community of Princess Ann. Today, the park headquarters, a picnic area, and a hiking trail extend along the bluff, which once served as a buffer against flooding for settlers. A boat ramp is conveniently located beside the camping area. Canoeists and kayakers launch their craft from here for short trips in the immediate area, or they use the ramp as a takeout, making shuttle runs upriver. This dark serpent of flowing watery wildness runs 115 miles, making overnight wilderness trips viable. Eighty-one of the river miles are designated as wild and scenic. If you don't have two cars for a shuttle, check the park office for a list of outfitters operating along the Lumber.

The Princess Ann Trail extends from the picnic area along the river and heads upstream for 1.5 miles. Check out Griffin's Whorl, where the Lumber reverses its flow before resum-ing downstream. Along the way, the path passes an observation deck and fishing pier. Folks angle here for crappie, sunfish, and largemouth bass. Bank fishing also takes place along the shore near the campground. I hope you will take the time to enjoy a tent-camping adven-ture here on the Lumber River.

Lumber River State Park: Princess Ann Access Campground

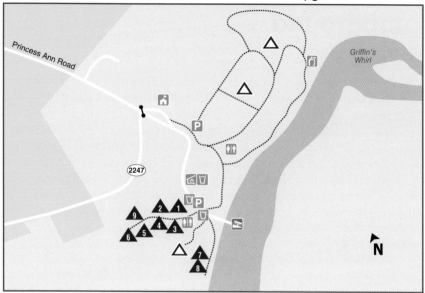

GETTING THERE

From Exit 13A on I-95 near Lumberton, North Carolina, take I-74/US 74/Andrew Jackson Highway east 13 miles to Creek Road (a sign for Orrum Middle School will be at this turn). Turn right on Creek Road, and follow it 5.3 miles. Turn left on Princess Ann Road, and follow it 2 miles to reach the Princess Ann Access of Lumber River State Park, on your left. The park's address is 2819 Princess Ann Road, Orrum, NC 28369.

GPS COORDINATES: N34° 23.303'   W79° 00.079'

31

Merchants Millpond State Park Campground

Beauty ★★★★★ Privacy ★★★★★ Spaciousness ★★★★ Quiet ★★★★★ Security ★★★★★
Cleanliness ★★★★★

Often overlooked, this is the jewel of the North Carolina state park system.

Merchants Millpond State Park is simply one of North Carolina's finest tent-camping destinations. This quiet getaway in the northeastern part of the state tends to be overlooked because it has neither the glamour of the ocean nor the lure of the mountains; nevertheless, this coastal-plain jewel shines brightly. The actual Merchants Millpond is a mini–Okefenokee Swamp, a brooding wetland ecosystem ideal for paddling and fishing in the relaxing quiet that only nature can provide. The surrounding high ground has its appeal, too, with many hiking trails traveling the land. To top it off, the campground seems to have been designed for tent campers.

As with all park facilities here, the campground is appealing and well maintained. It is laid out in a classic loop with a mere 20 campsites. Overhead, loblolly pines tower above red and white oaks, maples, and thick understory brush such as myrtle oak. Pine needles carpet the forest floor, and shade is abundant. Elevated tent pads make staking your tent easy and allow for quick drainage in case of rain. The campsites are located far from one another,

Water tupelo and bald cypress trees bring fall colors to Merchants Millpond State Park.

KEY INFORMATION

CONTACT: 252-357-1191; ncparks.gov /merchants-millpond-state-park

OPEN: Year-round

SITES: 20

EACH SITE HAS: Tent pad, picnic table, fire ring, lantern post

WHEELCHAIR ACCESS: Yes

ASSIGNMENT: First come, first served and by reservation (877-722-6762; ncparks.gov /make-reservation)

REGISTRATION: Ranger will come by to register you

AMENITIES: Hot showers, water, flush toilets

PARKING: At campsites only; 2 vehicles/site

FEE: $15–$23

ELEVATION: 25'

RESTRICTIONS:

PETS: On leash only

FIRES: In fire rings only

ALCOHOL: Prohibited

OTHER: 6 people/site; gates closed 6–9 p.m. (depending on season) to 8 a.m.

---

which, coupled with the thick woods, makes for maximum privacy. Most sites are on the outside of the loop, but here every site is a winner, no matter where it is located. Small trails lead to the center of the loop, where a nice bathhouse lies. Most sites can accommodate a large tent and screen shelter, if you so desire.

Spring and fall are the best times to visit Merchants Millpond. Summer can be hot and buggy. Late March through April and mid-October are the busiest times, though sites are available just about any weekend. Winter is quiet. Park gates are locked every evening until sunrise, making for maximum safety. A park ranger lives on-site.

Bennetts Creek was dammed more than 180 years ago, forming Merchants Millpond. The elevated pond provided waterpower to operate a gristmill and later a sawmill in Gates County. The 760-acre pond, ringed with cypress and gum trees, is filled with fish and other wildlife. Lassiter Swamp occupies the upper reaches of Bennetts Creek and the millpond. Canoes—for touring the swamp or casting a line to catch bream, crappie, or largemouth bass—are available for rent at very reasonable prices. Only electric motors are allowed on the lake, making it a quiet nature retreat. There are even backcountry canoe campsites for the adventurous. Check the park website for canoe-rental rates and information.

The park can also be explored by land. Several foot trails course through the woods and along the wetlands. One trail even has a campsite for backpackers. If you hike no other path, at least check out Cypress Point Trail, which makes a 0.25-mile loop along the edge of the millpond, overlooking the swamp from a boardwalk. Coleman Trail extends 2 miles. It offers good views of the millpond, travels through several habitats, and is a good birding

courtesy of North Carolina Division of Parks and Recreation

Paddlers explore the park's watery backcountry.

trail, especially during spring and fall migrations. Lassiter Trail, the master path of the park, can be picked up directly from the campground via a 0.4-mile spur trail. Make the 5-mile loop by passing along the north side of the millpond and along Lassiter Swamp. A park fire road cuts the loop in half. Park programs are held on weekends and will help inform you about this special swath of the coastal plain, which plainly, you should not miss.

Merchants Millpond State Park Campground

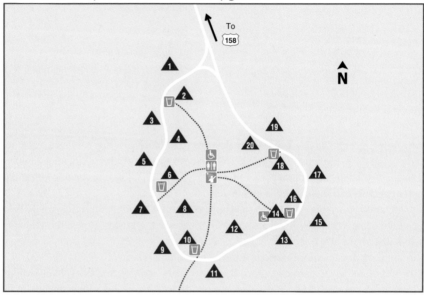

GETTING THERE

From Exit 173 on I-95 in Weldon, North Carolina, head east on US 158. In 2.1 miles, turn left on US 158/US 301. Go 2.4 miles and stay right on US 158. Go 39.8 miles, and exit onto US 13 N/US 158. In 6.7 miles, take right on US 158. Go 10.1 miles to the park, located on your right, west of Sunbury. The park's address is 176 Millpond Road, Gatesville, NC 27938.

GPS COORDINATES: N36° 26.721'   W76° 41.654'

32

Neuse River Campground
(ALSO KNOWN AS FLANNERS BEACH)

Beauty ★★★★ Privacy ★★★ Spaciousness ★★★★ Quiet ★★★ Security ★★★★ Cleanliness ★★★

This national forest campground offers water and land recreation on a tidal river.

Also known as Flanners Beach, this revamped bluff-side campground on the lower Neuse River is a fine recreation destination. The campground has been a beloved recreation spot for locals, as well as those who have come to know its charm. A paved hiking and biking trail loops through the campground. Flanners Beach, a sandy shoreline along the tidally influenced lower Neuse River, has been a swimming and waterside recreation destination for as long as people have been coming to have fun on this slice of coastal Carolina.

The campground is laid out in a loop. As you pass the campground host, there for your security, tall loblolly pines reach for the sky above an understory of smaller oaks and sweet gums. You will immediately notice that the campground has a landscaped look, as opposed to random tree growth. Live oaks, willows, and many other trees were planted, especially between campsites, to add privacy. Whether it returns to a completely natural look over time is irrelevant because the vegetation adds to the attractiveness of the Neuse River. As it is, the first several campsites in the loop have electricity, attracting the big rigs. But let not your heart be troubled, as 19 out of 41 sites are nonelectric. The sites on the inside of the

A beach along the lower Neuse River

KEY INFORMATION

CONTACT: Croatan Ranger District, Croatan
National Forest, 252-638-5628;
www.fs.usda.gov/recarea/nfsnc
/recarea/?recid=48466

OPEN: Year-round

SITES: 41

EACH SITE HAS: Picnic table, fire grate, lantern post; 24 have electricity

WHEELCHAIR ACCESS: Yes

ASSIGNMENT: First come, first served and by reservation (877-444-6777; recreation.gov)

REGISTRATION: Self-registration

AMENITIES: Hot showers, water spigots,
flush toilets

PARKING: At campsites only

FEE: $12; $17 electric

ELEVATION: 30'

RESTRICTIONS:

PETS: On leash only

FIRES: In fire rings only

ALCOHOL: Prohibited

OTHER: 14-day stay limit

The author hiking the Neusiok Trail

loop have more shade and vegetation than those on the outside, but they are smaller as well. A trip or two around the loop will reveal a mixture of sunny and shady spots. Several sites are close to the river, but the high bluff prevents quick access to Flanners Beach. Sites are generally available on all but summer-holiday weekends, and always during the week. A fine bathhouse centers the loop and is easily accessible to all campers.

The area encompassing the Croatan National Forest has a long history. Its name was likely derived from the Croatan people, who settled in villages along the Neuse River. The nearby town of New Bern, North Carolina's second oldest, was founded in 1710. Timber from the area became important in the production of tar. Later, small farms were established but were bought out, along with larger holdings, to establish the Croatan National Forest in 1936 for timber management and watershed protection. Recreation areas were developed over the decades, including Neuse River Campground. An errant mapmaker decided to name the campground after the nearby Neuse River, but the name has never caught on, and locals call the area Flanners Beach to this day.

A paved recreation trail is open to cyclists and hikers. It winds through the thick woods of the Neuse River bluff, about 30 feet above the river, and a tupelo swamp. A paved trail also connects the campground to an appealing picnic area where towering pines and hardwoods shade a grassy lawn. Wooden steps lead down to Flanners Beach. The tan sand, littered with driftwood, extends several yards in each direction, making for ample sunning and relaxing room (I enjoyed looking over the water here). No alcoholic beverages are allowed at the swim beach and picnic area.

The Neuse at this point is more of a bay than an inland river. Anglers can cast a line for striped bass, sunfish, largemouth bass, flounder, and crappie. The nearest boat ramp in the Croatan is at Cahooque Creek. Croatan National Forest offers other recreation opportunities on the tidal estuaries and freshwater lakes. Hikers can tackle the 26-mile Neusiok Trail, which crosses the 161,000-acre forest. On the way in to the campground, stop at the ranger station for more information. You can buy supplies back in New Bern.

Neuse River Campground (Flanners Beach)

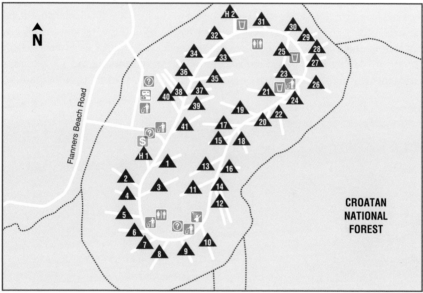

GETTING THERE

From the intersection of US 17 and US 70 in New Bern, North Carolina, head east on US 70, and go 6.6 miles. Keep left to stay on US 70, and go another 10.4 miles, 2 miles beyond the Croatan Ranger Station, on your left. Turn left on Flanners Beach Road, and follow it 1.5 miles to reach the campground.

GPS COORDINATES: N34° 58.875'   W76° 56.850'

33

⛺ Ocracoke Campground

Beauty ★★★ Privacy ★ Spaciousness ★★ Quiet ★★★★★ Security ★★★★ Cleanliness ★★★

This island campground is accessible only by car ferry.

Ocracoke Island is accessible only by ferry, but the extra effort reaps scenic rewards. Most of the island is part of the Cape Hatteras National Seashore and is kept in its natural state. The village of Ocracoke is a worthy destination. It evokes a 1950s fishing hamlet, with its cottages, narrow streets, and lack of franchise operations. The natural setting, the village, and the campground combine to make a relaxing getaway worth visiting for a few days or more.

The campground is the least inviting thing on the island, but it will suffice as your headquarters for exploring Ocracoke. The 135 campsites are in a flat behind dunes that separate you from the beach and the Atlantic Ocean. Most of the sites are on the main loop, which is broken by three crossroads; the sites on the inside of the loop are small and close together. Some small cedars and other trees, pruned back by the relentless wind, dot the otherwise-grassy campground. The loop curves around to reach the so-called dune sites, which are larger and are a short walk toward the beach from the paved parking pad. Other sites have average tent areas directly by the parking pad. Even the dune sites are open to the sun.

Dunes overlook the Atlantic Ocean.

KEY INFORMATION

CONTACT: Cape Hatteras National Seashore, 252-473-2111; nps.gov/caha; ferry: 800-293-3779; ncdot.gov/divisions/ferry

OPEN: Mid-April–late November

SITES: 135

EACH SITE HAS: Picnic table, upright grill

WHEELCHAIR ACCESS: Yes

ASSIGNMENT: First come, first served and by reservation (877-444-6777; recreation.gov)

REGISTRATION: At campground entrance booth

AMENITIES: Cold showers, water spigots, flush toilets

PARKING: At campsites only; 2 vehicles/site; must be parked on paved surface

FEE: $28

ELEVATION: 20'

RESTRICTIONS:

PETS: On leash only

FIRES: In upright grills only

ALCOHOL: At campsites only

OTHER: 6 people and 2 tents/site; 14-day stay limit in a 30-day period Memorial Day–Labor Day

The loop curves away from the beach. The sites here, located away from the water but still an easy walk to the beach, back up to a wetland, which can be problematic if the mosquitoes are biting. The sites on the loop crossroads are mostly flat, grassy, and open to the sun. Three separate restroom areas with cold showers are spread throughout the campground.

Reservations can be made in advance, but you cannot pick out a specific site. A timely arrival is recommended even with a reservation, especially on weekends. Reservations are highly recommended on holiday weekends and early July–mid-August. Be aware that mosquitoes can be a problem after wet spells, so mosquito repellent and a screen shelter will make your stay much more enjoyable. Furthermore, if you are taking the Cedar Island ferry or the Swan Quarter ferry, it's also wise to make reservations for your arrival and departure, especially during the busy season. I recommend coming during the shoulder seasons, when the crowds are gone, the village of Ocracoke is in really low gear, and the better campsites are available.

Life is slow on Ocracoke Island. You can sense it as you walk the beach. A great place for quiet walks is the beach-access area across from the pony pens (more about those later). No cars are allowed on the beach here, and no development can be seen. (Cars are allowed on the beach near the campground.) Sea kayaking is popular on the Pamlico Sound side of the island, and boats of all sorts can be rented in the village of Ocracoke (supplies can be purchased here as well). You can also rent bikes for pedaling around the village, charter a sport-fishing boat, eat in a unique restaurant (no franchises allowed!), visit the Ocracoke Lighthouse (built in the early 1800s), or just sit back on a bench at Silver Lake Harbor and watch the boats come and go. Take the Ocracoke Historical Interpretive Trail to learn about the lengthy past of this land. This place really does have character.

The ponies that once roamed Ocracoke are now taken care of by the park service. They are quartered a few miles from the campground. The animals are thought to have swum ashore from a Spanish shipwreck long ago. An interpretive trail travels near the horse pens. Another interpretive trail, Hardwood Hammocks Trail, travels into the island interior. The path starts just across the road from the campground. Start your planning now for a trip to Ocracoke Island.

Ocracoke Campground

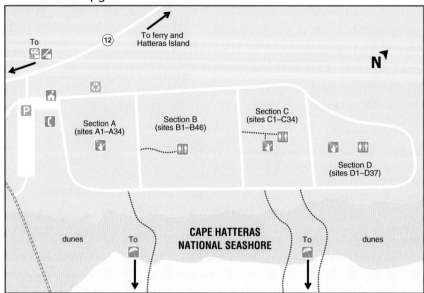

GETTING THERE

From the intersection of US 64 and US 158 just south of Nags Head, North Carolina, drive south on NC 12 for 58.8 miles, and turn right to take the ferry at the southwest end of Hatteras Island. Take the free ferry over to Ocracoke Island. Once off the ferry, keep south on NC 12 for 9.5 miles to reach the campground, on your left. Two other, longer toll-ferry options reach Ocracoke Island as well; for more information, call 800-293-3779, or visit ncdot.gov/divisions/ferry. The campground's address is 4352 Irvin Garrish Highway, Ocracoke, NC 27960.

GPS COORDINATES: N35° 07.615'   W75° 55.145'

SOUTH
CAROLINA
UPCOUNTRY

Vista from atop Table Rock *(see campground 38, page 126)*

34

Cherry Hill Campground

Beauty ★★★★★ Privacy ★★★★ Spaciousness ★★★★★ Quiet ★★★★ Security ★★★★ Cleanliness ★★★★★

Cherry Hill is South Carolina's finest Upcountry campground.

Cherry Hill Campground is the focal point for the Cherry Hill Recreation Area. And as one of the best national forest campgrounds in the Southern Appalachians, it is a fine place to be. The campground, in the shallow upper valley of West Fork Creek, lies covered with an abundant understory beneath a towering forest of hardwood and pine. Just off SC 107 is the entrance to the campground. Immediately to the left is a circular turnaround, known as the overflow area. It once was home to a settler, whose chimney still stands just off the loop; a

Miuka Falls on the Winding Stairs Trail

KEY INFORMATION

CONTACT: Andrew Pickens Ranger District, Sumter National Forest, 864-638-9568; www.fs.usda.gov/scnfs

OPEN: April–October

SITES: 29

EACH SITE HAS: Picnic table, fire pit, lantern post

WHEELCHAIR ACCESS: Yes

ASSIGNMENT: First come, first served and by reservation (877-444-6777; recreation.gov)

REGISTRATION: Self-registration

AMENITIES: Hot showers, water, flush toilets

PARKING: At campsites only

FEE: $15

ELEVATION: 2,250'

RESTRICTIONS:

PETS: On leash only

FIRES: In fire pits only

ALCOHOL: At campsites only

OTHER: 6 people/site; 14-day stay limit

---

short path leads to the ruins. Four campsites have been carved into the woods there, but you must park on the loop and carry your belongings a few feet to these sites.

The main campground lies beyond the overflow area on a short spur road that descends to tranquil West Fork Creek. Just past the self-service pay station are two sites isolated on their own miniloop. A water spigot is nearby. Three other sites are off the spur road before you reach the main loop, which makes a large oval beside the West Fork.

All the sites along the West Fork are shrouded in rhododendron and are ideal for campers who like deep, lush woods. Four relatively open sites are on the inside of the main loop and offer a generous amount of space for even the most gear-laden camper. The sites away from the West Fork back against a hill beneath more open woods. Three water spigots are situated throughout the main loop. A clean, well-kept comfort station is at the north end of the loop; it has warm showers and flush toilets. There are no electric hookups.

Near the comfort station, a small circular drive splits off the main loop. It holds four campsites with large parking areas, apparently designed for RVers, who were the only campers I saw at that spot during my visit. The circle has its own water spigot.

A campground host is stationed at Cherry Hill and keeps the place immaculate and safe. This only adds to the relaxing atmosphere of the area. Just as you get really comfortable, a notion will strike you to venture beyond your folding chair to explore more of the beauty of Sumter National Forest. And you don't even have to leave Cherry Hill to walk some of the area trails. For starters, try Cherry Hill Nature Trail. It leaves the campground and makes a 0.5-mile loop among the ferns and brush of the white-pine forest.

Winding Stairs Trail also leaves from the campground. Follow it down as it switchbacks through an oak forest along the south side of the West Fork. This gentle switchbacking led to the Winding Stairs name. After a mile, you'll come to Miuka Falls, as West Fork Creek has picked up some volume on its way to merge with Crane Creek. After the fall, Winding Stairs Trail veers south to Crane Creek, passing Secret Falls after 2.3 miles, then returns to West Fork only to end at 3.5 miles on Forest Service Road 710.

If you want bigger water, the Chattooga, a Wild and Scenic River, is only a stroll away on Big Bend Trail. The trail starts just across SC 107 from the campground and leads 2.7 miles west into the protected corridor of the Chattooga 0.8 mile upstream of Big Bend Falls. From there, trails lead along the river in both directions for miles. Either way you go, you'll soon understand why this border river between South Carolina and Georgia is protected. The flora, fauna, and tumbling white water are yours to appreciate. The fishing's good too.

Cherry Hill is a great campground in an attractive forest setting. Get all your supplies back in Walhalla because, once you're at Cherry Hill, you won't want to spoil your vacation with an early return to civilization.

Cherry Hill Campground

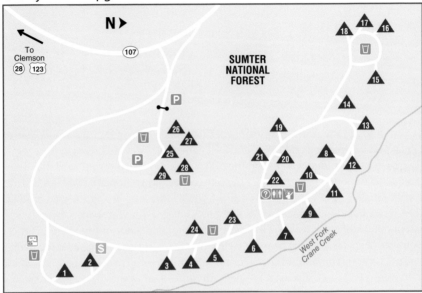

GETTING THERE

From I-85, take Exit 1, and head north on SC 11. Go 19.7 miles, and turn left on SC 28. Go 9.4 miles to SC 107; then turn right. Follow SC 107 for 8.5 miles. The entrance to Cherry Hill Campground will be on your right.

GPS COORDINATES: N34° 56.560'   W83° 05.280'

35

Devils Fork State Park Campground

Beauty ★★★★ Privacy ★★★ Spaciousness ★★★ Quiet ★★★ Security ★★★★★ Cleanliness ★★★★

Enjoy walk-in sites that overlook South Carolina's most beautiful lake.

Have you ever seen Lake Jocassee? Others may disagree, but I believe this impoundment to be South Carolina's most beautiful lake. A richly forested shoreline overlooks emerald water against a backdrop of the Blue Ridge Mountains. On the lake's northern shores are the Jocassee Gorges—steep valleys where waterfalls are created by cool, clear streams. Devils Fork State Park occupies some of Lake Jocassee's awesome shoreline, abutted by walk-in tent sites and affording instant water access.

Being a water-oriented park, the campground is, unsurprisingly, near the shoreline. Even better, the walk-in tent sites are close to the lake. The main tent-camping area spurs onto a wooded peninsula extending into the lake, with a paved trail leading down to the campsites. Descend along a rib ridge covered in mountain laurels, oaks, pines, and tulip trees. Sites T-1–T-8 dip toward the lake but are closer to the parking area. The mountain slope has been leveled at each site. Sites T-9–T-15 overlook the water and offer a view of the mountains beyond the lake. Landscaping timbers have been installed at the sites and beyond to slow erosion. Sites T-16–T-19 are too close to one another but overlook the lake;

Paddler's-eye view of Lake Jocassee

KEY INFORMATION

CONTACT: 864-944-2639;
southcarolinaparks.com/devils-fork

OPEN: Year-round

SITES: 25 walk-ins, 59 others

EACH SITE HAS: Walk-ins have tent pad, picnic table, fire ring; others also have electricity and water

WHEELCHAIR ACCESS: Yes

ASSIGNMENT: First come, first served and by reservation (866-345-7275; reserve.south carolinaparks.com/devils-fork)

REGISTRATION: At park office

AMENITIES: Hot showers, water spigots, flush toilets, laundry

PARKING: At walk-in parking area and at campsites; 2 vehicles/site; $10/additional vehicle/day; must park on paved surface

FEE: $19–$36 walk-ins; $23–$45 others

ELEVATION: 1,150'

RESTRICTIONS:

PETS: On leash only

FIRES: In fire rings only

ALCOHOL: Prohibited

OTHER: 6 people/walk-in site; 40' RV-length limit

T-18 is the best of this bunch. Site T-20 is closest to the walk-in parking area. The least appealing sites here are T-6, T-8, and T-19, but they are still better than most sites at other campgrounds. A water spigot lies at the beginning of the walk-in-camper access trail.

A second set of walk-in tent sites is accessible from the day-use area, near a playground. Take a short gravel path to reach sites T-21–T-25, where the woods are more open. Site T-22 is near the lake. Sites T-23 and T-24 are a little too close together. Site T-25 has the farthest walk but ends up near some of the drive-up sites in the main campground area. A water spigot is near these sites.

The main drive-up campground has two loops. Trees shade the sites, and ample vegetation screens them from one another. Most have tent pads. Any of these sites will suffice, but the tent sites are far more desirable. And because all sites are reservable, why not go for the ones you like? Reservations are strongly recommended, as the campground fills nearly every weekend from Easter through fall.

This park is fairly small but has two hiking trails. The 1.5-mile Oconee Bells Nature Trail takes you by places where the rare Oconee bell wildflower grows. Bear Cove Trail makes a 3.5-mile loop and starts at the day-use area. Most recreation is focused on this beautiful lake. You'll see

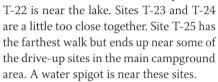

Enjoy trails like this one near Lake Jocassee.

campers swimming near their sites, as no supervised swim area exists. Watercraft access to the lake is made easy at the park boat ramp. If you don't have a boat or you want to get shuttled across the lake to explore some of the Jocassee Gorges, Jocassee Outdoor Center is just outside the park. It has fishing gear and bait; rents motorboats, canoes, and kayaks; and offers shuttles, guided sightseeing, and fishing and waterfall tours on Lake Jocassee. Visit the website at jocasseeoutdoorcenter.com.

Lake Jocassee is worth seeing. You can check out all the rivers that feed it from gorges coming out of the mountains—Whitewater River, Devils Fork Creek, Horsepasture River, and Toxaway River. I have explored them via the Foothills Trail, which runs along the north shore of Lake Jocassee, and proclaim them a prize resource of both North and South Carolina. Make a reservation to tent camp at Devils Fork and explore Lake Jocassee; then see if you, too, think it is South Carolina's most beautiful lake.

Devils Fork State Park Campground

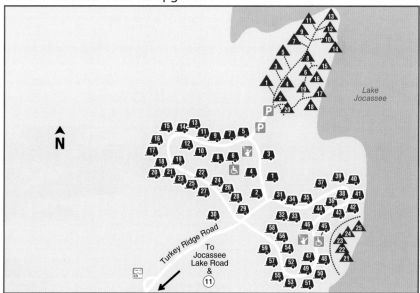

GETTING THERE

From I-85, take Exit 1, and head north on SC 11. Follow it 34.2 miles, and turn left on Jocassee Lake Road. Go 3.5 miles to reach the park, on your left. Turn left on Devils Fork Road, and go less than 0.5 mile to reach the campground on your right. The park's address is 161 Holcombe Circle, Salem, SC 29676.

GPS COORDINATES: N34° 57.482'   W82° 57.233'

36

Jones Gap State Park Campground

Beauty ★★★★★ Privacy ★★★★ Spaciousness ★★★ Quiet ★★★★★ Security ★★★★★ Cleanliness ★★★★

South Carolina operates this ecological treasure more sensitively than most other state parks.

This state park and the adjacent Caesars Head State Park are operated as low-impact wilderness parks. This means that they are not designed like traditional parks with big drive-up campgrounds, parking lots, and heavy usage areas. Rather, the park facilities are integrated into an exceptional mountain landscape, leaving the emphasis on the natural. Foot trails lead along crystalline streams beneath cathedral-like forests, where rock faces offer sweeping vistas and spring wildflowers peek through leaves that colored the landscape the previous fall.

For tent campers, low impact means carrying your stuff to rustic walk-in tent campsites and treading lightly on the land. It means packing your trash not only from your campsite but also from the entire park. It also means giving in to the spell the park puts on you, so that no matter what time of year you visit, it will make you want to return for more hiking through the Mountain Bridge Wilderness Area and for taking in more of the sights.

The hiking trails at Jones Gap State Park feature incredible vistas such as this one.

KEY INFORMATION

CONTACT: 864-836-3647;
southcarolinaparks.com/jones-gap

OPEN: Year-round

SITES: 9 walk-ins

EACH SITE HAS: Fire ring

WHEELCHAIR ACCESS: No

ASSIGNMENT: First come, first served and
by reservation (866-345-7275; reserve.south
carolinaparks.com/jones-gap)

REGISTRATION: At ranger station

AMENITIES: Hot showers, water spigots,
flush toilets (all at the parking area)

PARKING: At walk-in-camper parking area;
2 vehicles/site

FEE: $9–$17, depending on season

ELEVATION: 1,500'

RESTRICTIONS:
PETS: On leash only

FIRES: In fire rings only

ALCOHOL: Prohibited

OTHER: No trash cans—pack it in, pack it
out; permit required

Jones Gap State Park offers 18 campsites. The nine described below are walk-in sites within 0.5 mile of the camper parking area. The other nine are considered backcountry campsites. To reach the walk-in sites, leave the camper parking area and cross a bridge over the Middle Saluda River, deservedly South Carolina's first designated scenic river. Ahead is the impressive log cabin that houses the park office and visitor center; this is where you register. If no one is there, follow the instructions on the park office door.

Now to the campsites. Sites 1–4 are located past the old fish-hatchery pool on Hospital Rock Trail, to your right as you face the visitor center. The paved trail leads to a dirt trail and the woods. Site 1 lies along a small streamlet among boulders in dark rhododendron. Shaded by oaks, site 2 is a little on the sloped side. Site 3 sits away from the water in a notch between two ridgelines, shaded by hickories and oaks. Site 4, near the pipeline that feeds the hatchery pool, overlooks a mountain ravine.

Sites 5–7 are close to the camper parking area. These lead into woods from a path just to the left of the visitor center, with the Middle Saluda nearby. Site 5 is up a hill on a neat, rocky flat. The numerous embedded boulders there act as camp furniture. Site 6 is in a flat directly beside the river. Site 7 lies at the end of this short trail, fewer than 100 yards from the visitor center. It is banked against a hillside near the river, shaded by rhododendron.

Sites 8 and 9 are up the Jones Gap Trail heading directly up the Middle Saluda from the camper parking area. Hardwoods surround large site 8. The noise of the river crashing over boulders will sing you to sleep. Site 9 is the hardest to reach, 0.4 mile from the parking area. It is large, too, and is also along the river. Rocks and sand form the site's floor.

The campsites fill on the first nice weekends in spring, and then visitors taper off when the heat rises. From mid-August until the leaves fall, the campsites can fill any weekend. During the week you can get a campsite anytime. The bathhouse, with a water spigot outside, is located near the visitor center and is open 24-7. The visitor center also has water spigots.

The picnic area near the visitor center and former hatchery area exudes tranquility. The mown grass contrasts with the verdant forests, steep mountains, and crashing river. You will wish you had a scenically located log cabin of your own. But visiting Jones Gap State Park is about hiking and exploring the Mountain Bridge Wilderness Area. Trails galore wind through the campground. One of my fondest outdoor memories occurred at Jones Gap. I hiked the entire Foothills Trail from Oconee State Park 90 miles to the park in fall. The final morning dawned cool and crisp as wood smoke curled from my fire. I walked down through The Winds (as in winding a clock) along the numerous cascades of the Middle Saluda, framed in autumn color. I enjoyed the satisfaction of completing the entire trail with such an inspiring ending.

Jones Gap has many other trails and destinations in addition to the river. The combined area of Jones Gap and adjacent Caesars Head State Parks is known as the Mountain Bridge Wilderness Area. A wilderness trail map, available at the park office, reveals much more than a weekend's worth of possibilities. Head to Raven Cliff Falls or Hospital Rock, or hike up Coldspring Branch to enjoy wildflowers. A shorter but challenging loop includes the Rim of the Gap Trail and returns via Little Pinnacle Mountain on the Pinnacle Pass Trail. Jones Gap is all about trails and wilderness; just remember to leave the land in this mountain treasure the way you find it.

Jones Gap State Park Campground

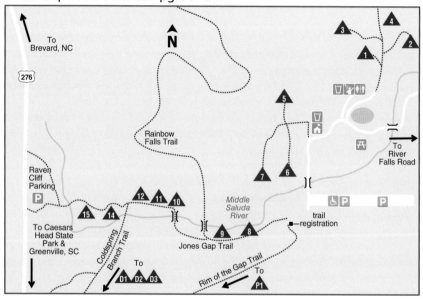

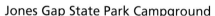

GETTING THERE

From the intersection of US 123 and SC 183 in Greenville, South Carolina, head northwest on SC 183/Buncombe Street, and go 0.2 mile. Turn right on US 276. Go 19 miles, and turn right on River Falls Road. In 4.6 miles keep straight as it turns into Jones Gap Road, and go 1.2 miles to dead-end at Jones Gap State Park. The park's address is 303 Jones Gap Road, Marietta, SC 29661.

GPS COORDINATES: N35° 07.588'   W82° 34.343'

37

Keowee–Toxaway State Park Campground

Beauty ★★★★ Privacy ★★★★ Spaciousness ★★★★ Quiet ★★★★ Security ★★★★★ Cleanliness ★★★★★

Cherokee heritage, scenic hill country, mountain lakes, and a peaceful campground make Keowee–Toxaway an outstanding state park.

This area of South Carolina is aptly named the Cherokee Foothills. The Cherokee thrived here long before white settlers ever laid eyes on the land. South Carolina recognizes this, and Keowee–Toxaway tips a hat to indigenous culture in the natural setting of the Cherokee Foothills at this quiet, well-maintained state park.

Tent campers can enjoy the area by day and return to a great campground at night. It is situated on a well-wooded knoll that tastefully integrates campsites with the steep terrain using well-placed landscaping timbers. Shade is abundant beneath the canopy of hickories and oaks, though a relatively light understory somewhat diminishes privacy.

Tent campers have their own separate loop. No loud generators will interfere with the sounds of chirping birds. The 14 tent sites are all spacious and level enough for setting up

You can catch a glimpse of Lake Keowee from the Raven Rock Trail.

KEY INFORMATION

CONTACT: 864-868-2605;
southcarolinaparks.com/keowee-toxaway

OPEN: March–December

SITES: 14 tent-only, 10 RV

EACH SITE HAS: Tent pad, picnic table,
fire ring with attached grill

WHEELCHAIR ACCESS: Yes

ASSIGNMENT: First come, first served and by
reservation (866-345-7275; reserve.south
carolinaparks.com/keowee-toxaway)

REGISTRATION: Ranger will come by to
register you

AMENITIES: Hot showers, water, flush toilets

PARKING: At campsites only

FEE: $9–$11; $16–$18 RV, depending
on season

ELEVATION: 1,000'

RESTRICTIONS:

PETS: On leash only

FIRES: In fire rings only

ALCOHOL: Prohibited

OTHER: 14-day stay limit on one campsite;
40' RV-length limit

a normal amount of gear, but expect some seriously sloping topography if you stray from your designated area. That slope, though, allows for balcony-like views into the hollows beyond the campground knoll. The sites on the inside of the loop are less steep beyond their timbered camping area. The tent pads at this state park are among the finest I have seen—they are slightly crowned in the center, allowing for quick runoff during those heavy mountain thunderstorms. This is just one more obvious sign that the campground is well designed.

Another plus is that you'll never have to go far for water. Three spigots are evenly distributed along the small loop. RVers and tent campers share a comfort station located between the two separate loops. Hot showers and flush toilets are provided. Additional features include firewood for sale at the park office and excellent campground safety. In fact, this might be the safest campground in the state. Park gates are locked at night, and the ranger residence is just a stone's throw away from the tenters' loop.

Near the park office is Keowee–Toxaway's centerpiece: the Cherokee Interpretive Center, which recognizes the area's Cherokee heritage. During my visit I learned quite a bit about native life before, during, and after the arrival of European settlers, and also about the flora and fauna that inhabit the state park. Visit the interpretive center first for an enhanced appreciation of the historic and natural life here.

Just outside the interpretive center is the 0.25-mile Cherokee Interpretive Trail. It winds through the woods and chronicles the evolution of the Cherokee tribe at four informative kiosks, culminating with the story of their removal from their ancestral lands along the infamous Trail of Tears.

Other, longer trails carpet the park. The 4-mile Raven Rock Trail undulates amid the piney hills and hardwood hollows along clear creeks to a rock cliff overlooking Lake Keowee, then loops back via the Natural Bridge Trail to the park's Meeting House. A rock bridge spans Poe Creek along the Natural Bridge Trail. The 0.7-mile Lake Trail leads from the campground down to the shore of Lake Keowee. This state park may be only 1,000 acres, but South Carolinians make the most of the scenic beauty packed into the small package.

Lake lovers have two nearby bodies of water to enjoy. Both Lake Keowee and Lake Jocassee back against the Blue Ridge, affording mountainous shorelines. Lake Keowee, the larger of the two, is a warm-water fishery, with bass and bream as its primary sport fish. Anglers will be surprised to find trout in Lake Jocassee's deep, cool waters. Nearby Devils Fork State Park on Lake Jocassee also offers good camping, with a special section of walk-in tent sites.

Overall, you will find the understated Keowee–Toxaway State Park a pleasant surprise. It is ideal for tent campers who want an intimate, well-kept campground with plenty of amenities. The blending of Cherokee heritage and natural beauty was a masterstroke by South Carolina park officials. Don't make the mistake of overlooking this small jewel of the Palmetto State.

Keowee–Toxaway State Park Campground

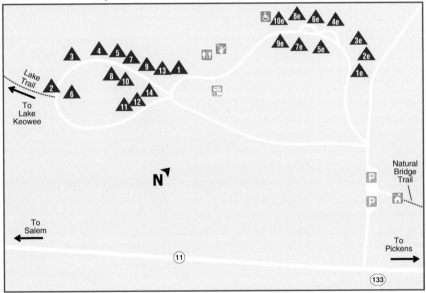

GETTING THERE

From the intersection of US 178 and SC 183 in Pickens, South Carolina, drive north on US 178 for 8.6 miles. Turn left on SC 11, and drive 8.6 miles to Keowee–Toxaway State Park. Turn right to reach the campground. The park's address is 108 Residence Dr., Sunset, SC 29685.

GPS COORDINATES: N34° 56.017′   W82° 53.315′

38

Table Rock State Park Campgrounds

Beauty ★★★ Privacy ★★★ Spaciousness ★★ Quiet ★★★ Security ★★★★★ Cleanliness ★★★★★

The wide variety of attractions at this state park will make your stay worthwhile.

The distinctive granite face of Table Rock Mountain has attracted people to this scenic area since the days of the Cherokee, who believed the Great Spirit dined on the mountain's flat top, hence the name Table Rock. Later, this area was developed by the Civilian Conservation Corps during the Great Depression. The Corps's handiwork was so well crafted that Table Rock Mountain State Park was placed on the National Register of Historic Places in 1989.

Not that this park needed man's imprint to be special. Waterfalls, deep forests, and rock outcrops adorned the mountains long before the 3,083 acres became a state park in 1935. The facilities just make it more user friendly.

Mountain Laurel Campground has 75 sites spread on a two-loop setup in open, rolling woods that have suffered the ravages of many storms, which have made pulp of the pine trees that once dotted the campground. In addition, little is left of the understory, minimizing privacy. It's strange to see a campground with electrical and water hookups at each site but no elaborate site shaping or defined tent pads. But don't let that scare you—only 20 of the sites are designated as pull-throughs, which translates to RVs. The six primitive walk-in sites offer seclusion and value for tent campers.

The first eight sites lie along the approach road and are very open. Campsites are placed fairly close together inside the loop. Three bathhouses with flush toilets and hot showers are evenly dispersed among the sites, the exception being the sites on the approach road. Degrees of sun, shade, and slope vary from site to site. Plenty of level, shaded sites are available. Expect the best ones to be taken during the weekends.

The primitive camping area is on the south side of SC 11, near the visitor center and park office. The sites here are set on a ridge near Lake Oolenoy. Pines shade the sites, which

A summer view of Table Rock

KEY INFORMATION

CONTACT: 864-878-9813;
southcarolinaparks.com/table-rock

OPEN: Year-round

SITES: 6 walk-ins, 94 others

EACH SITE HAS: Walk-ins have tent pads,
picnic tables, and fire rings; others also
have water and electricity

WHEELCHAIR ACCESS: Yes

ASSIGNMENT: By reservation (866-345-
7275; reserve.southcarolinaparks.com
/table-rock)

REGISTRATION: At camp store or at Table
Rock visitor center

AMENITIES: Hot showers, water, flush toilets (no access for walk-ins), camp store,
laundry, Wi-Fi

PARKING: At campsites only

FEE: $17 walk-ins; $25 others

ELEVATION: 1,160'

RESTRICTIONS:

PETS: On 6' or shorter leash only

FIRES: In fire rings only

ALCOHOL: Prohibited

OTHER: 14-day stay limit; 40' RV-length limit

---

are a 500-plus-foot walk. Site 1 is on a slope, but 2 is set above it. Sites 3 and 4 are together and are the best shaded. Sites 5 and 6 are highest on the hill. Water and a pit toilet are located on a trail near the six sites.

Located in thicker woods on a dead-end road, the White Oaks Campground area may actually be preferable to the Mountain Laurel Campground if you like less hustle and bustle. Its 25 sites are spread along a loop and share a single bathhouse with flush toilets.

At Table Rock, the campground is just a place to rest and eat between activities. Two lakes lie within the park's confines. Pinnacle Lake finds summertime campers relaxing on its beach or jumping off the high and low diving boards into the clear, cool waters. Canoeists fish for bass, bream, or catfish, and pedal boaters take scenic rides atop the lake's 36 acres.

If water is not your thing, get together with the full-time park naturalist. Many programs are offered during summer. The Table Rock Nature Center has displays that detail the natural history of the region. Children can have fun at the playground.

The best way to enjoy these South Carolina mountain lands is on foot. A 10-mile trail network emanates from the nature center. The 3.4-mile Table Rock Trail lives up to its national recreation trail status. It leads upward among giant boulders to Pinnacle Ridge at Panther Gap. From Panther Gap, the trail climbs the steps of Governor's Rock (which offers a view) to reach the top of Table Rock at 3 miles. Hike another 0.5 mile to enjoy more views of the South Carolina countryside.

Pinnacle Mountain Trail is very challenging. It passes Mill Creek Falls and Bald Knob on the way to the 3,425-foot peak, the park's highest point. A 2-mile connector trail links Pinnacle Mountain and Table Rock Trails. Carrick Creek Nature Trail offers a shorter 1.8-mile loop through forest characteristic of this worthwhile park. Every path here is a winner.

GETTING THERE

From the intersection of US 178 and SC 183 in Pickens, South Carolina, drive north on US 178 for 8.6 miles. Turn right on SC 11, and follow it 4.1 miles. Turn left on West Gate

Road, and go 0.5 mile. Turn right on Table Rock State Park Road. The park's address is 158 East Ellison Lane, Pickens, SC 29671.

GPS COORDINATES: N35° 01.588'   W82° 42.217'

Table Rock State Park: Mountain Laurel Campground

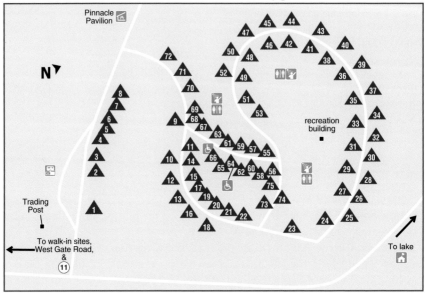

Table Rock State Park: White Oaks Campground

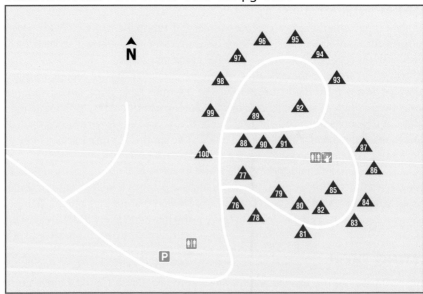

SOUTH CAROLINA MIDLANDS

Parsons Mountain Lake *(see campground 44, page 145)*

39

Brick House Campground

Beauty ★★★ Privacy ★★ Spaciousness ★★★★ Quiet ★★★★ Security ★★★ Cleanliness ★★★

This quiet campground is a base for those traveling the Buncombe Horse Trail or paddling nearby streams.

Talk about transition—one minute I was zipping along I-26, and the next I was at Brick House Campground. The place was so quiet that I could hear myself breathe. Rushing down the interstate was exactly what I was trying to escape. The serene atmosphere and quaint natural setting of Brick House are exactly what tent campers want. Brick House delivered, so much so that I just hung around the campsite all day reveling in the clear,

The Buncombe Horse Trail starts next to the Brick House Campground.

KEY INFORMATION

CONTACT: Enoree Ranger District, Sumter
  National Forest, 803-276-4810;
  www.fs.usda.gov/scnfs

OPEN: Year-round

SITES: 23

EACH SITE HAS: Picnic table, fire ring;
  most also have lantern posts

WHEELCHAIR ACCESS: Yes

ASSIGNMENT: First come, first served;
  no reservations

REGISTRATION: Self-registration

AMENITIES: Vault toilets

PARKING: At campsites only; 2 vehicles/site

FEE: $5

ELEVATION: 450'

RESTRICTIONS:

PETS: On leash only

FIRES: In fire rings only

ALCOHOL: At campsites only

OTHER: 14-day stay limit for some sites

crisp fall air that had swept over the South Carolina Midlands. The next day I hiked the nearby Buncombe Horse Trail. A mountain bike would've been an even better means of traveling this trail, but I was regrettably bikeless. However, mountain bikers are discovering and enjoying this path in ever-increasing numbers.

The Enoree District of the Sumter National Forest is just a short drive up I-26 from Columbia. So it makes sense that the Buncombe Horse Trail is catching on. But the lack of use at Brick House Campground is surprising. Sure, a few equestrians, hunters, and family campers find their way here, but this place can be a nice base camp for trail enthusiasts too. Despite being only 4 miles from the interstate, Brick House seems a world away.

After passing the Buncombe Horse Trailhead, enter the campground loop, where tall pines form the forest canopy. Elms, dogwoods, sweet gums, and other hardwoods grow beneath the taller evergreens. The forest floor is littered with pine needles and pointy sweet gum balls.

There is little brush between campsites, but privacy isn't as much of an issue as you would think. Because this campground rarely, if ever, fills, you likely won't have a neighbor next to you. Sites 1 and 2 are close together and act as a double site. The woods are sparse behind these camps due to cutting from a pine-beetle infestation, but most pines in the campground loop have been spared. The water spigot has been dismantled, so bring your own water. Come to large, open sites on the outside of the loop. A stone marker for the Youth Conservation Corps, which rehabilitated this campground and Buncombe Horse Trail, sits next to the road. Site 12 is purely in pines. Curve around to reach the shady sites.

Notice the white-banded trees near some sites. These are where occasional horse campers can tie their animals. The terrain slopes away from the campground as the loop turns back toward Brick House Road. Some open sites lie on the inside of the loop. Come to a group of three shady sites at the campground's end. This is where I stayed, in 23. Two vault toilets serve the campground.

You may notice blue blazes on trees running behind site 13. This is the Buncombe Horse Trail. You can pick it up there or start at the trailhead, located just a short piece down Brick House Road, which you passed on the way in. The Buncombe Horse Trail, open to hikers, mountain bikers, and equestrians, is broken into colored segments of different lengths. It circles the Headleys Creek watershed through environments typical of the Piedmont. The

Red Trail cuts across the main loop, allowing two loop trips of 9 and 12 miles, respectively. Hikers, mountain bikers, and equestrians are welcome to enjoy this trail. Trail maps are posted at signboards in the campground and at the trailhead. South Carolina's master path, Palmetto Trail, runs in conjunction with part of the Buncombe Horse Trail. I've hiked nearly the entire trail system. Bring your hiking boots and a two-wheeler to double your fun at this first-rate spring and fall Midlands destination.

Don't forget your canoe or kayak. You can paddle the Tyger or Enoree River, both of which flow nearby through the national forest. With all there is to do, Brick House is a regular stop in my Palmetto wanderings.

Brick House Campground

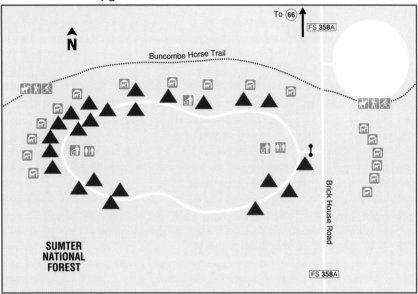

GETTING THERE

From Exit 60 on I-26 near Clinton, South Carolina, head northeast on SC 66 for 3.6 miles. Turn right on Brick House Road/Forest Service Road 358, and follow it 0.5 mile to reach the campground, on your right.

GPS COORDINATES: N34° 26.717'   W81° 42.427'

40

Calhoun Falls State Park Campground

Beauty ★★★★ Privacy ★★★★ Spaciousness ★★★★ Quiet ★★★★ Security ★★★★★ Cleanliness ★★★

The awesome walk-in tent sites here should serve as models for other parks to follow.

Don't look for some big waterfall when you come to this lakeside recreation area. Before the damming of Richard B. Russell Lake, the Savannah River once flowed free. At high water, a rapid on the Savannah River, near where the Calhoun family resided, resembled a waterfall. Now, Calhoun Falls is just the name of a town and a nearby state park centered on large Richard B. Russell Lake. The U.S. Army Corps of Engineers developed this impoundment, the middle of three consecutive large reservoirs damming the Savannah River. Part of the Corps's work was on Calhoun Falls State Recreation Area, which it turned over to the South Carolina state park system to manage. The walk-in tent sites here should serve as models for other parks to follow.

High-quality campsites are costly to build, and the Corps of Engineers spared no expense here. This is evident in the fixtures of every campsite you see, with first-rate fire grates, picnic tables, lantern posts, and more. The walk-in tent sites are near Campground 2. The first set of walk-in sites comprises T-5–T-0 (you reach the sites in reverse order).

This walk-in tent site overlooks Russell Lake.

courtesy of DiscoverSouthCarolina.com

KEY INFORMATION

CONTACT: 864-447-8267;
southcarolinaparks.com/calhoun-falls

OPEN: March–December

SITES: 14 walk-ins, 84 others

EACH SITE HAS: Walk-ins have tent pad,
picnic table, fire ring, lantern post, and
cooking table; others also have electricity
and water

WHEELCHAIR ACCESS: Yes

ASSIGNMENT: First come, first served and by
reservation (866-345-7275; reserve.south
carolinaparks.com/calhoun-falls)

REGISTRATION: At tackle shop

AMENITIES: Hot showers, water spigots,
flush toilets, vault toilets, laundry

PARKING: At walk-in-camper parking area
and at campsites; 2 vehicles/site

FEE: $17 walk-ins; $23–$27 others, depend-
ing on season

ELEVATION: 500'

RESTRICTIONS:

PETS: On 6' or shorter leash only

FIRES: In fire rings only

ALCOHOL: Prohibited

OTHER: 14-day stay limit;
30'–40' RV-length limit

Dip into thick woods and a streamside hollow. T-5 is in a flat beside the hollow. Landscaping timbers have been laid into the hillside to level the campsites, which have a sand floor. Cross two footbridges to reach T-4, which is very shady and has a walkway to the lake. The path leaves the hollow and reaches sites overlooking an arm of the lake. T-3 is more open but is shaded by water oak, cedar, and a few other trees. Bring a canopy during midsummer for sun protection. T-2 directly overlooks the water. T-1 is set on a point; shade is limited, but the water panorama is appealing. T-0, over a hill, offers maximum solitude. The walk from the parking area to T-0 is about 140 yards.

The second walk-in area is home to sites T-6–T-13, located on the upper end of a cove. T-6 and T-7 are so close to the parking area as to almost lose their walk-in status. That is not to say they are bad—they aren't. The camps are directly on the water. T-8 and T-9 are also on the water but are more shaded. T-10 has easy access to the parking area but not to the lake. T-11 is thickly shaded but is off the lake. Cross footbridges to reach T-12. Shaded and on the water, it is highly recommended. T-13, another shady site, is the farthest from the parking area. A path from T-13 leads to the water. All sites here, including the walk-in tent sites, are reservable. Oddly, the walk-in sites generally fill only on holiday weekends. An outdoor shower, water spigots, and vault toilets are in the immediate campground vicinity. Tent campers can use the showers at the other campgrounds.

Two other large campgrounds, Campground 1 and Campground 2, serve the park. They are leveled, landscaped, and well thought out, mixing pull-through sites with pull-up sites for RVs and tent campers who wish to have on-site water and electricity. A look at these two lakeside camping areas shows that no expense was spared here either.

The developed recreation areas are nice too. The beach house for the lake's swim area is beyond elaborate for a park structure. Tennis courts and a basketball court are located near the beach house. Cedar Bluff Nature Trail leaves from near the beach house and makes a 1.75-mile loop.

Most of the other recreation opportunities center on Russell Lake (named after a Georgia politician). The recreation area has its own marina, boat ramp, dock, and tackle shop.

The Savannah River forms much of the border between South Carolina and Georgia. Russell Lake covers 26,000 acres, plenty of room to enjoy the water sport of your choice. If you don't have a boat, you can cast your line from one of the two park fishing piers. One is located near the walk-in area by site 56 of Campground 2. The other pier is by the boat ramp. Just remember that one water feature you won't see at this fine destination is a waterfall.

Calhoun Falls State Park Campgrounds

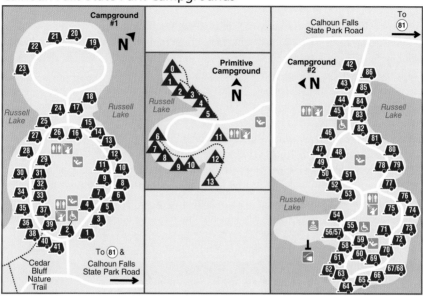

GETTING THERE

From the intersection of SC 71 and SC 28 in Abbeville, South Carolina, head south on SC 28, and go 2.9 miles. Turn right on SC 72 W, and go 12.8 miles to the town of Calhoun Falls. Turn right on SC 81, and follow it 1.1 miles. Turn left on Calhoun Falls State Park Road, and continue more than 1 mile to enter the state park and reach the various camping areas. The park's address is 46 Maintenance Shop Road, Calhoun Falls, SC 29628.

GPS COORDINATES: N34° 06.430'   W82° 36.985'

41

Kings Mountain State Park Campground

Beauty ★★★ Privacy ★★★ Spaciousness ★★★★ Quiet ★★★ Security ★★★★★ Cleanliness ★★★★

This large state park complements an adjacent Revolutionary War battlefield.

Did you know that more Revolutionary War battles took place in South Carolina than in any other state? Take the Battle of Kings Mountain, which took place on October 7, 1780, and is considered the turning point for the Americans in the South. Frontiersmen from North Carolina, South Carolina, Tennessee, and Virginia gathered to defeat Lord Cornwallis and end the British advance into North Carolina. The Loyalists and English army were forced to retreat back to Charleston, ultimately to lose the war. Today, you can visit this battlefield, known as Kings Mountain National Military Park, and pitch your tent at the adjacent Kings Mountain State Park, which functions as the recreational counterpart to the battlefield. Here, you can hike, swim, fish, and enjoy yet more American history beyond the battlefield.

Campsites at the state park are widespread among pines and oaks. As you pass the Trading Post, a small campground store, the ridgetop camping area slopes away from the main campsites. The first large loop has 75 sites, which are shared by tent campers, pop-ups, and RVs. The second major loop has the balance of the sites, including walk-in tent sites. The

A log cabin on the living-history farm

KEY INFORMATION

CONTACT: 803-222-3209; southcarolinaparks.com/kings-mountain

OPEN: March–December

SITES: 10 walk-in, 109 full hook-up

EACH SITE HAS: Walk-ins have tent pad, picnic table, and fire ring; others also have electricity and water but no tent pad

WHEELCHAIR ACCESS: Yes

ASSIGNMENT: First come, first served and by reservation (866-345-7275; reserve.south carolinaparks.com/kings-mountain)

REGISTRATION: At campground Trading Post April–October; ranger will come by to register you rest of year

AMENITIES: Hot showers, water, flush toilets, laundry

PARKING: At walk-in tent parking and at campsites; 2 vehicles/site

FEE: $13–$16 walk-ins; $17–$30 others

ELEVATION: 750'

RESTRICTIONS:

PETS: On 6' or shorter leash only

FIRES: In fire rings only

ALCOHOL: Prohibited

OTHER: 14-day stay limit; 40' RV-length limit

tent campers' parking area is near site 82. Beyond the parking area and along the loop, sites are far enough in the woods to lend a rustic atmosphere, but not so far back that you'll feel like a mine mule after setting up camp. The understory is much thicker among the tent sites, with brush and smaller trees complementing the shady forest. Descend along a ridgeline between two narrow hollows to find site T-1, which is closest to the parking area. T-2 and T-3 are next to a dry streambed. A trail leads past T-4. As the loop begins to curve back uphill, reach T-5, which is a bit sloped. T-6, set among many pines, has a water spigot near it. I would be proud to pitch my tent at T-7 or T-8. The loop curves back toward the parking area, making sites T-9 and T-10 easily accessible.

A campground host assists campers during the warmer months. Numerous bathhouses are evenly spread among the loops, including one near the tent campers' parking area. A recreation building at the campground makes rainy days more livable. The campground sees the most traffic during spring and fall but only fills on major summer holidays. The campground also sees some traffic from I-85 travelers, but walk-in tent campers can nearly always get a site.

The state park offers 7,000 acres, which, combined with the 3,000 acres of the military park, make for a lot of roaming space in the shadow of Charlotte. Two lakes add to the attractive park terrain. Lake Crawford covers 15 acres. Lake York is larger at 65 acres and offers johnboats, pedal boats, and canoes for rent, so anglers can vie for bass and bream. Bring your own canoe or kayak to paddle either lake. Basketball and volleyball courts are near the campground.

I really enjoyed the hiking trail that connects the state park to the military park. The path makes a 16-mile loop and has backcountry campsites amid its ridges and bottomlands, where clear streams flow. I have made this loop in a day. Though rewarding, it will challenge you. You can bite off bits and pieces of the trail, as there are multiple auto-accessible trailheads. If you don't feel like walking to the nearby Kings Mountain battlefield, just make a stop at the visitor center to check out the museum and a video explaining the battle. Then take the 1.5-mile, self-guided loop trail around the battlefield and appreciate one of many Revolutionary War sites in South Carolina, which has more than any other state.

Kings Mountain State Park Campground

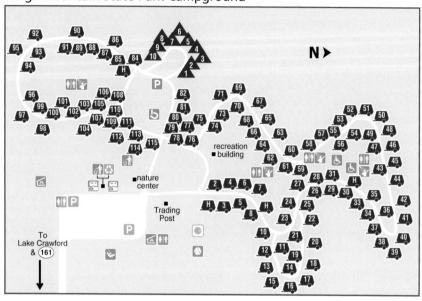

GETTING THERE

Take I-85 to Exit 8 for Kings Mountain just north of the North Carolina–South Carolina border, and head south on NC 161 for 4.8 miles, leaving North Carolina en route. Turn right on Park Road, and follow it into the state park. In 1 mile turn right on Lake Crawford Road to reach the campground. The park's address is 1277 Park Road, Blacksburg, SC 29702. Do not rely on digital mapping for directions.

GPS COORDINATES:

N35° 08.965'   W81° 20.833'

A trailside vista at the adjacent Kings Mountain National Military Park

42

⛺ LeRoys Ferry Campground

Beauty ★★★ Privacy ★★★★★ Spaciousness ★★★★ Quiet ★★★ Security ★★★ Cleanliness ★★★

This is the most primitive campground on the shores of Thurmond Reservoir.

The shores of Thurmond Reservoir abound with campgrounds. While scouring them for this book, I found that most were just too big and overly developed. But on arriving at LeRoys Ferry, I knew that it was a winner. It was small, primitive, and quiet compared with other campgrounds. The ones that didn't make the cut resembled campground cities, strung out along the shore with signs pointing me here, there, and everywhere while I searched for good sites. I even got lost in the campground of one unmentioned state park along the lake. After that experience, small LeRoys Ferry seemed like home. Its simplicity was a relief.

Simple is the watchword here. This U.S. Army Corps of Engineers campground is more about what it doesn't have than what it does have. For starters, it doesn't have a ranger station, confusing signs, hordes of bustling campers, or cars and trailers constantly coming and going. Furthermore, it doesn't have much to do in the way of organized recreation. There are no trails to hike or bike, no nature centers, no boats to rent, and no fishing piers. The only amenity, in addition to the campground, is a boat launch. You have two choices here: make your own fun on Thurmond Reservoir or just relax at the campground, which is a fine thing in itself. And for $10 a day, the price is right. Making your own fun could also

A spillway release at Thurmond Reservoir

courtesy of U.S. Army Corps of Engineers

CONTACT: Savannah District, U.S. Army Corps of Engineers, 800-533-3478; www.sas.usace.army.mil/lakes/thurmond

OPEN: Year-round

SITES: 10

EACH SITE HAS: Picnic table, fire grate, lantern post; most sites have upright grills

WHEELCHAIR ACCESS: No

ASSIGNMENT: First come, first served; no reservations

REGISTRATION: Self-registration

AMENITIES: Pump well, vault toilets

PARKING: At campsites only

FEE: $10

ELEVATION: 340'

RESTRICTIONS:

PETS: On leash only

FIRES: In fire rings only

ALCOHOL: At campsites only

OTHER: 14-day stay limit

include bank fishing or swimming on the shoreline. String up a hammock and bring that book you always wanted to read. Spend some face-to-face time with family and friends—another difficult task when phones infiltrate more and more of our everyday lives.

Just because this campground is primitive doesn't mean that it's not well kept. The Army Corps of Engineers generally takes good care of its property, which ultimately belongs to us. Reach the end of the dead-end road, and pass the fee station that is near the pump well. A gravel road leads right 0.25 mile to campsites 4–1 (you reach the sites in reverse order). The hillside slopes toward the lake, but the sites are mostly level. Site 4 is large and overlooks the lake. Site 3 is a good distance away in thick woods. Pine grows highest above these sites, followed by a thick bank of winged elm and oak. Easy-to-identify sweet gum trees rise in dense rows throughout the campground. The straight-trunked trees thrive in moist soils. Its star-shaped leaves turn a deep maroon color in autumn. However, its most notable features are the spiny balls that fall in huge numbers to the point of being a nuisance in yards. Smaller trees and brush create more than ample privacy. Site 2 is less shady. Site 1 is close to the lake.

Loon on Thurmond Reservoir

photographed by Eric Haskell US Army Corps of Engineers Savannah District

Return to the main road that shortly splits. The paved road leading left dead-ends at the boat ramp. A second gravel road that splits right has sites 10–5. Site 10 is large and closest to the boat ramp. Site 9 is well above the lake, while sites 8 and 7 are separated by thick woods yet are open toward Thurmond Reservoir. I stayed in site 6 because it provided good afternoon shade on a hot summer day. Site 5 is at the road's end. Informal trails lead a short distance from these sites to the lake. Despite having only 10 sites, the campground fills only on holiday weekends. Other than then, you should get a site. Interestingly, the campground was closed for a period due to budget concerns, but public demand led to its reopening.

People come here for fishing, boating, skiing, and swimming. And Thurmond Reservoir is a huge recreation destination. Completed in 1954 and named after the late US Senator J. Strom Thurmond, the lake now hosts 7 million visitors annually. But it doesn't seem that way at LeRoys Ferry. After all, a tent camper can still find a little solitude along the 1,200 miles of shoreline here. Plus, more than 100 islands add a scenic touch to the impoundment. It seems the lake also has 100 campgrounds, but you will likely find that the few sites at LeRoys Ferry offer the best in tent camping.

LeRoys Ferry Campground

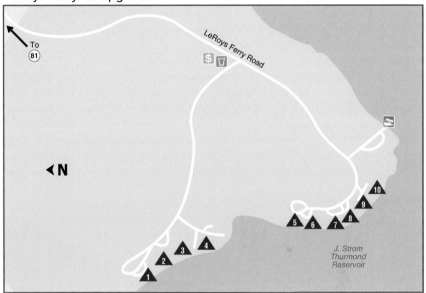

GETTING THERE

From the intersection of US 221 and US 378 in McCormick, South Carolina, head southwest on US 221, and go 0.5 mile. Turn right on SC 28/North Mine Street, and go 6.9 miles. Veer left, staying with SC 81 N, and go 5.5 miles to the hamlet of Wilmington. Turn left at the signed turn for LeRoys Ferry Campground, going just a few feet over defunct railroad tracks; then immediately turn right on S-33-196. Go 0.5 mile; then turn left on Willington Academy Drive/S-33-135, and follow it 1.6 miles. Keep right and go 2 miles on LeRoys Ferry Road to dead-end at the campground.

GPS COORDINATES: N33° 55.327'   W82° 29.452'

43

Lick Fork Lake Campground

Beauty ★★★★ Privacy ★★★ Spaciousness ★★★ Quiet ★★★★ Security ★★★★ Cleanliness ★★★

This little valley campground seems a world away from the surrounding area.

Campgrounds and recreation areas with lakes come in all sizes. Lick Fork Lake is a mere 12 acres, small compared with most impoundments, especially compared with nearby Lake Thurmond. Lick Fork Lake Campground has only 10 sites—just about the right number to handle this lake. Located in the surprisingly deep and secluded valley of Lick Fork (but only 10 miles from a town), the area exudes a close, intimate feel, as if you are in the middle of nowhere. The no-gas-motors rule on the lake, along with the widespread campsites, means that chirping birds and maybe some kids swimming in the clear water will be your only background noise.

I really like this campground. The sites are spacious and spread out far from one another. They are incorporated into a hilly setting with some leveling and stonework that make the sites both attractive and "campable." Oaks and pines provide the shade. A gravel road dips toward Lick Fork Lake, passing a water spigot to reach sites 1 and 2. These are on mostly level terrain. Sand has been spread in individual camping areas, each with a separate tent pad. Sites 3–5 are built into a slope. Landscaping stones held together with concrete form leveling walls, resulting in two-tiered sites. As the gravel road curves toward the lake, reach site 6, which overlooks the lake from across the road. Then come to

View of Lick Fork Lake

KEY INFORMATION

CONTACT: Long Cane Ranger District, Sumter National Forest, 803-637-5396; www.fs.usda.gov/scnfs

OPEN: May–November

SITES: 10

EACH SITE HAS: Tent pad, picnic table, fire ring

WHEELCHAIR ACCESS: Yes

ASSIGNMENT: First come, first served; no reservations

REGISTRATION: Self-registration

AMENITIES: Cold showers, vault toilets (day-use area: water, flush toilets)

PARKING: At campsites only

FEE: $7

ELEVATION: 350'

RESTRICTIONS:

PETS: On leash only

FIRES: In fire rings only

ALCOHOL: At campsites only

OTHER: 14-day stay limit

the most favored sites, 7–9. These directly overlook Lick Fork Lake, which is just a short downslope walk away. Site 9 is on a point just above the lake's fishing pier. The road then curves away from the lake into a hollow. The final site here, 10, is usually occupied by the campground host.

The campground, with so much area for so few sites, has four vault toilets. The small number of sites means that it fills quickly at times, especially on weekends during late spring and early summer. Then the heat kicks in and business dies down. Sites are available during the week any time of year. A campground host is on duty most of the warm season and locks the campground gate at 10 p.m., a plus for camper security.

A restroom with cold showers overlooks the swim and picnic area. The picnic shelter here is a nice place to hang out during a summertime thunderstorm. Elaborate stonework has leveled parts of the picnic area, which overlooks a grassy lawn adjacent to the roped-off swim area. The latter has a sandy bottom for clean-footed entry into and exit out of the pretty lake. A paved walkway with a quaint bridge connects the picnic area to a small fishing pier and the boat launch (as previously mentioned, no gas motors are allowed here). Anglers vie primarily for catfish but also largemouth bass and bream. The clear water and deep valley remind me of a small mountain lake rather than a lake in the South Carolina Midlands.

Two trails emanate from the boat-launch area. The Lick Fork Trail circles

Jack-in-the-pulpits

around the lake, making a 2-mile circuit that emerges from the woods near the swim area. The Horn Creek Trail is longer, at 5.7 miles. Mountain bikers really enjoy this route, though it sees its share of hikers as well. The path leaves the Lick Fork drainage, then climbs over a ridge to dip into the Horn Creek drainage. From here, the path winds along Horn Creek before returning. It crosses forest roads three times, helping you track your progress. And Horn Creek may be about as far away as you want to get from this hideaway, tucked in the little valley of Lick Fork.

Lick Fork Lake Campground

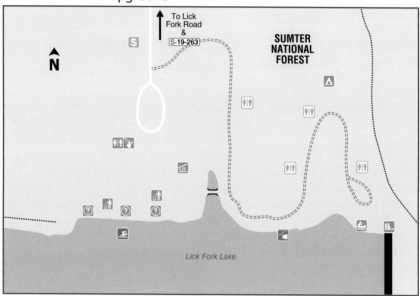

GETTING THERE

From I-20, take Exit 1, and head north on SC 230. In 16.9 miles turn right on Lick Fork Road/S-19-263. Follow it 2 miles to the campground, on your right.

GPS COORDINATES: N33° 43.760'   W82° 02.443'

44

Parsons Mountain Lake Campground

Beauty ★★★★ Privacy ★★★★ Spaciousness ★★★★ Quiet ★★★★ Security ★★★ Cleanliness ★★★

Tent campers will love this excellent national forest recreation area.

Parsons Mountain Lake Recreation Area, in Sumter National Forest, offers boating, swimming, fishing, and hiking, along with an excellent campground in a rustic and well-kept setting. One goal of the U.S. Forest Service is to manage our national forests for public recreation. It is for this reason that areas like Parsons Mountain are developed. Under the multiple-use concept, the Forest Service also manages lands for watershed protection, timber harvesting, and wildlife enhancement, among other things. Tent campers benefit greatly from the recreation component of the multiple-use concept.

The roots of the recreation area were planted decades ago, when the Civilian Conservation Corps dammed Mountain Creek and developed the resulting shoreline, including the campground. The historic part of the recreation area, stonework and such, was left intact. You will pass the day-use area before entering the campground. Campsites 1 and 3 are on an arm of Parsons Mountain Lake and are the only lakeside sites here. Oddly, these sites are lesser used than those in the main campground. Sweet gum, dogwood, pine, cedar, and elm

The author looks out on Parsons Mountain Lake.

KEY INFORMATION

CONTACT: Long Cane Ranger District, Sumter National Forest, 803-637-5396; www.fs.usda.gov/scnfs

OPEN: May–November 15

SITES: 23

EACH SITE HAS: Tent pad, picnic table, fire grate, lantern post

WHEELCHAIR ACCESS: Yes

ASSIGNMENT: First come, first served; no reservations

REGISTRATION: Self-registration

AMENITIES: Showers, flush toilets, vault toilets

PARKING: At campsites only; 2 vehicles/site

FEE: $7

ELEVATION: 475'

RESTRICTIONS:

PETS: On leash only

FIRES: In fire rings only

ALCOHOL: Prohibited

OTHER: 14-day stay limit

compose the forest overhead. Continue beyond a picnic area to enter the main part of the campground, on a hillside loop.

Starting with campsite 4, the sites are large. They are well separated from one another and have ample young trees between them for privacy. Overhead shade from taller trees varies with the sites but is adequate at each camping area. Site 10 is of special note, as it is the most isolated. Most sites on the loop's outside are set back in the woods; a bathhouse centers the loop. Site 17 is closest to the bathhouse. A short trail connects the main loop to the day-use area near site 20. A campground host is on duty during the warm season.

Twenty-three sites is a desirable number for a campground. The size keeps the campground generally quiet, but not so small that it fills too quickly. However, Parsons Mountain does fill on ideal spring and early summer weekends.

At 28 acres, Parsons Mountain Lake is also just the right size. The shoreline is pretty everywhere you look, whether it is the grassy picnic areas shaded by tall pines or the trees growing along the shoreline. No gas motors are allowed, and boaters will be pleased to know that the lake has a boat ramp, making boating or fishing for largemouth bass, bream, and catfish easy. An earthen pier on one side of the lake is where bank fishermen will be found. The primary day-use area has a designated swim beach downhill from the modern bathhouse. This area also has a large picnic shelter, which is a good place to take cover during summer thunderstorms.

The lake is not the only draw here, though. The Tower Trail leads from near the lake spillway 1.2 miles to the top of Parsons Mountain, where a fire tower stands. This out-and-back hike has a 400-foot elevation change, a big change in these parts, and offers a varied forest-scape along the way. Unfortunately, the fire tower is closed. You can also see evidence of Civil War–era gold mining along the trail. The Parsons Mountain OHV Trail, open to hikers, mountain bikers, and motorized vehicles, makes a 12-mile loop south of the recreation area. It can be accessed by keeping east on Parsons Mountain Road, beyond the turn into the campground to Forest Service Road 515. Turn right on FS 515 to reach the trailhead past the road to the fire tower.

Parsons Mountain Lake Campground

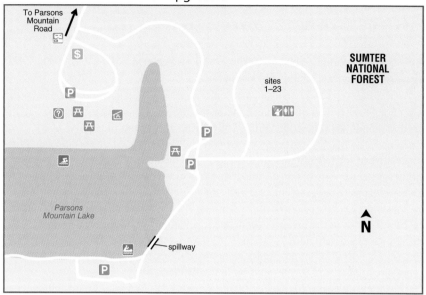

GETTING THERE

From the intersection of SC 71 and SC 28 in Abbeville, South Carolina, head south on SC 28, and go 5.1 miles. Turn left on Parsons Mountain Road, and follow it 1.4 miles. Turn right on Campground Road, and follow it 0.8 mile to reach the campground.

GPS COORDINATES: N34° 06.188'   W82° 21.343'

45

Poinsett State Park Campground

Beauty ★★★★★ Privacy ★★★★ Spaciousness ★★★ Quiet ★★★ Security ★★★★ Cleanliness ★★★★

This state park is one of South Carolina's most ecologically interesting areas. It offers great camping, mountain biking, and hiking too.

Poinsett State Park has an interesting location. Set on an outlier of the Carolina Sand Hills, Poinsett is where the vegetation of the Lowcountry meets the vegetation of the Upstate, resulting in the overlapping of ecosystems—a place where Spanish moss hangs in trees that stand over blooming mountain-laurel bushes. The melding of nature's finery results in a beautiful setting for a park, and an understanding of why this was an early addition to the South Carolina state park system, originally developed by the Civilian Conservation Corps (CCC) in the 1930s. Historic structures from the CCC era add charm to an already pretty place. Another plus in the location department is Poinsett's proximity to Manchester State Forest, which effectively adds thousands of acres to the activity area, where hiking and mountain-biking trails abound. Add a camping loop used exclusively by tent aficionados, and you have a great outdoor destination in the Palmetto State.

The campground is set high on a hill, but the sites, laid out in a classic double loop, are mostly level up here. Pines, oaks, sweet gums, dogwoods, and hickories, draped in Spanish moss, stand over sandy sites. Ample ground vegetation divides the sites and provides good privacy. Two bathhouses serve the locale.

Spillway at Old Levi Mill Lake

KEY INFORMATION

CONTACT: 803-494-8177;
southcarolinaparks.com/poinsett

OPEN: Year-round

SITES: 50

EACH SITE HAS: Picnic table, water spigot,
fire ring; 24 have electricity and water

WHEELCHAIR ACCESS: Yes

ASSIGNMENT: First come, first served and by
reservation (866-345-7275; reserve.south
carolinaparks.com/poinsett)

REGISTRATION: At park office by lake

AMENITIES: Hot showers, water, flush toilets, Wi-Fi

PARKING: At campsites only; 2 vehicles/site

FEE: $12–$15; $16–$22 electric

ELEVATION: 185'

RESTRICTIONS:

PETS: On 6' or shorter leash only

FIRES: In fire rings only

ALCOHOL: Prohibited

OTHER: 6 people/site; 40' RV-length limit

The first loop, the original one, has electric sites. Also note the rock fire rings from the CCC days in the first few sites. The second loop, at the back of the campground, is where tent campers want to be. The loop once had electricity, but it was taken out. However, each site still has its own water spigot. The large, shady sites allow room for all the extras you can cram in your vehicle. A few sites have tent pads, but the sandy floors already make for a level, easy-draining surface. The campground road circles around to pass by a large field, then reenters the first loop. Note the recreation building here, which could come in handy during rain spells.

Campsites are always available in the nonelectric loop; however, make reservations for peace of mind. Once you come here, in fact, you can find the site you like and reserve it for the next trip. Poinsett is a spring and fall destination: summer can be excessively hot, and there is no swimming here. Note: You may experience noise from a nearby military bombing range.

The CCC dammed Shanks Creek to create 10-acre Old Levi Mill Lake. The scenic, watery valley offers boating and fishing in a quiet setting where gas motors are not allowed. You can rent a johnboat, pedal boat, canoe, or stand-up paddleboard from the park or bring your own canoe, kayak, or other boat, as long as you can carry it to the water because there is no boat launch. Private boats must be 14 feet long or less. Bass, bream, and catfish lie beneath the placid pond.

Most campers travel the extensive trail system that spreads over the state park and Manchester State Forest. South Carolina's master path, the Palmetto Trail, which extends from the mountains to the sea, heads through here in what is known as the High Hills of Santee Passage. This segment of the Palmetto Trail is 14 miles long from end to end.

The Coquina Trail makes a loop around Old Levi Mill Lake, which connects to another loop trail, the Hilltop Trail, which in turn connects to the Laurel Group Trail. The Equestrian Trail, also open to hikers, makes a 6-mile loop among valleys cut by spring-fed creeks. Swamp vegetation, such as tupelo and cypress, grows next to mountain vegetation, such as galax and mountain laurel, on the hills.

On the way in, you pass the main mountain-biking trailhead for the 25,000-acre Manchester State Forest, which has trails aplenty. Three trails make loops covering more than

17 miles of pedaling. The K3 Trail is the longest, at 10 miles. Be prepared for some of the hilliest terrain in this part of the state and also for sand, as you are in the sandhills. Some riding can be quite technical. The trails are closed at times during the fall hunting season, so consider coming in spring for more riding opportunities. Also, a permit is required to bike the trails. To obtain a permit online, visit www.state.sc.us/forest/permit.htm. This way, you will be prepared for your visit to Poinsett State Park.

Poinsett State Park Campground

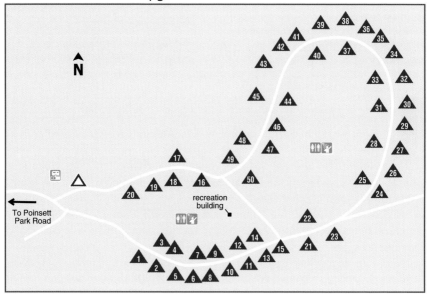

GETTING THERE

From Exit 9A on I-77 in Columbia, South Carolina, turn right and head east on US 378/US 76/Garners Ferry Road. Go 26 miles, and turn right on SC 261. Drive 10.1 miles, passing through Wedgefield. Turn right on Poinsett Park Road at the signed turn, and go 1.7 miles to enter the state park. The park's address is 6660 Poinsett Park Road, Wedgefield, SC 29168.

GPS COORDINATES: N33° 48.477'   W80° 32.000'

46

⛺ Sand Hills State Forest Campground

Beauty ★★★ Privacy ★★★★ Spaciousness ★ ★★★★ Quiet ★★★ Security ★★★ Cleanliness ★★★

This unusual ecosystem offers camping and recreation galore.

A prehistoric sea once covered what is now South Carolina, depositing sand over a wide area. Later, these seas retreated, leaving a region of deep, infertile hills of sand. Over time, many plants and animals adapted to these hills, but settlers farming the land couldn't thrive as nature could. The state eventually acquired the land and now manages 46,000-acre Sand Hills State Forest. Here, tent campers can enjoy the activities of the forest, such as mountain biking, hiking, fishing, and exploring the unique ecosystem.

You get to camp on a hill so big that it's called a mountain—Sugarloaf Mountain. Height is relative here at the edge of the Midlands, but there are scenic views toward the coastal plain in parts of the forest.

Enter the campground via Mountain Road, dipping to Mountain Pond, a small but pretty impoundment of 10 acres. To your right are two large picnic shelters made of wood and stone, flanked by campsites 1A and 1B. Campers can use these rustic shelters, which overlook Mountain Pond. Oaks, dogwoods, and pines shade the sites, though the trees are widely separated in the area. Cross over the pond dam. Site 2 has a shelter and also overlooks the lake. Begin to climb Sugarloaf Mountain, passing sites 3 and 4 on the left. Reach the upper end of the mountain, where three more sites with shelters lie between

Take a hike in the Sand Hills State Forest.

photographed by John Richburg

KEY INFORMATION

CONTACT: South Carolina Forestry Commission, 843-498-6478; www.state.sc.us /forest/refshill.htm

OPEN: Year-round

SITES: 16

EACH SITE HAS: Picnic table, trash barrel; some also have covered shelters

WHEELCHAIR ACCESS: No

ASSIGNMENT: Reservations required (843-498-6478)

REGISTRATION: At forest headquarters

AMENITIES: Vault toilets

PARKING: At campsites only

FEE: $10 sites without shelters; $15 sites with shelters

ELEVATION: 325'

RESTRICTIONS:

PETS: On leash only

FIRES: In fire rings only

ALCOHOL: Prohibited

OTHER: 14-day stay limit

Sugarloaf and Horseshoe Mountains. (These so-called mountains are really large hills, which can be climbed via erosion-preventing wooden stairs placed on the hillsides.) Site 7 offers excellent solitude.

The second camping area, with sites 8–15, is available for equestrian groups and tent campers. It is more open and sandy. (Be aware that tent campers are encouraged to use the first seven sites rather than the equestrian area.) Sites 8 and 9 are in a loop beside Mountain Pond. The remaining sites are in a large loop amid sandy pinewoods. All are very large and offer great privacy and more room than anyone would ever need to pitch a tent. The sites with shelters are the most popular. The only other campground amenity is vault toilets, so bring your own water.

Campsites can be reserved, although the campground traditionally fills only on holiday weekends. Spring and fall are the most popular use periods. Note that you need a trail permit from the forest office for mountain biking, but not for hiking. Call ahead and you can have your permit mailed to you, or you can pick it up at the forest headquarters.

Nearly all campers climb Horseshoe and Sugarloaf Mountains as a matter of course. Pick up the trailhead of Long Trail, a 1.7-mile nature path, by leaving Mountain Pond and walking toward SC 29, the way you came in. Others will try their luck fishing in Mountain Pond, where bream and bass ply the waters. The state forest has 13 other fishable ponds, but mountain biking is what's really going on here.

Sand Hills State Forest has established a mountain-biking trail that starts near its headquarters and offers 11 miles of biking over four loops, the largest of which is 6 miles. Screamer, Vista, and Ho Chi Minh Trails are some names that sections of the bike trail have received. Cyclists and other visitors can also enjoy the adjacent Carolina Sandhills National Wildlife Refuge, where 100 miles of gravel roads await. These roads are only occasionally used by park personnel and are "edging toward singletrack," according to the park. Hiking and driving trails also await. I enjoyed driving around the state forest. (Truth be known, I got lost trying a shortcut. Get a map at forest headquarters before you explore and don't rely on handheld devices for navigation.) Nonetheless, I was surprised at the views and the attractive nature of this land. It has so much potential, and with a campground like Sugarloaf Mountain, your base camp is set and waiting for you.

Sand Hills State Forest Campground

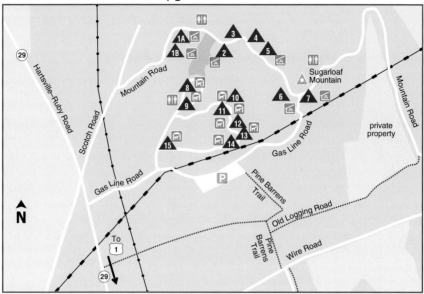

GETTING THERE

From Columbia, South Carolina, take I-20 E to Exit 98. Head north on US 521, and go 2.5 miles. Turn right on US 1, and go 36.8 miles. (The state forest headquarters is 0.8 mile farther along US 1, on the left.) Turn left on Hartsville–Ruby Road/Forest Service Road 29, and follow it 2.8 miles. Turn right on sandy FS 63/Scotch Road, which leaves at an angle, and follow it 0.5 mile. Veer right on Mountain Road, and reach the camping area with sites 1–7. The second area (sites 8–15) is off Gas Line Road, which heads to the right from Hartsville–Ruby Road/FS 29 just before Scotch Road.

GPS COORDINATES: N34° 35.213'   W80° 07.753'

47

Woods Ferry Campground

Beauty ★★★ Privacy ★★★ Spaciousness ★★★★ Quiet ★★★★ Security ★★★ Cleanliness ★★★

This part of the Sumter National Forest is rich in river recreation.

Like the rest of South Carolina, Woods Ferry Recreation Area is loaded with American history. The adjacent Broad River was an obstacle to travelers of times past. In 1817 Matthew Woods saw an opportunity, acquiring the land that is now the campground and constructing a ferry for people, horses, and buggies to cross the truly broad river. During the Civil War, Confederate General Wade Hampton used the ferry while chasing Union General William Sherman during the latter's infamous March to the Sea, which effectively ended the War between the States. Later, the terrain, like much of the South Carolina Midlands, was logged and then unsoundly farmed, leading to soil erosion. The U.S. Forest Service took over the depleted lands, managing them for timber and recreation. Bridges replaced the ferry both north and south of its former location. Today, Woods Ferry, a rustic recreation area with a quiet campground, offers hiking, boating, and fishing.

Johnny paddles the Broad River near Woods Ferry.

KEY INFORMATION

CONTACT: Enoree Ranger District, Sumter National Forest, 864-427-9858; www.fs.usda.gov/scnfs

OPEN: Year-round (November–March: no showers)

SITES: 17

EACH SITE HAS: Picnic table, fire ring; lantern post

WHEELCHAIR ACCESS: Yes

ASSIGNMENT: First come, first served; no reservations

REGISTRATION: Self-registration

AMENITIES: Hot showers, water spigots, flush toilets, vault toilets

PARKING: At campsites only

FEE: $7

ELEVATION: 400'

RESTRICTIONS:

PETS: On leash only

FIRES: In fire rings only

ALCOHOL: At campsites only

OTHER: 14-day stay limit

The campground is situated along a sloping valley beside the Broad River. The valley, moister than the area uplands, flourishes in a forest of oaks, elm, and cedars, with a small understory of trees and bushes. Reaching Loop A first, pass the first two sites as the loop angles up the hillside. The sites here are large. Reach a high point at site 10, which is a double. The loop then curves past a small bathhouse with hot showers that is walled on the sides but open to the sky. The loop flattens out and ends at site 17. Water spigots are seemingly everywhere in this campground.

Loop B, which is closer to the Broad River than Loop A, has camping units 18–30 but is closed unless needed for overflow.

Boaters use Woods Ferry occasionally, as do hunters, but overall the place is underused. This is a make-your-own-fun campground. My fun started with the day-use area. Located on a flat beside the Broad River, this area has the right combination of sun, shade, grass, and covered picnic shelters (handy in the rain) for enjoying the Broad River.

A boat ramp is used by those with johnboats, kayaks, and canoes floating the Broad. You can put in here and travel 6 or 7 miles downstream to the South Sandy boat ramp. A U.S. Forest Service map comes in handy here, so order one before your trip. The nearby Tyger and Enoree Rivers are excellent for paddling, with clear water and narrower, more intimate streamsheds. The Tyger offers 24 miles of floating, while the Enoree offers 36 miles of paddling through the national forest. All three rivers offer freshwater angling.

Also, the Woods Ferry area has a trail system used by hikers, mountain bikers, and horses. Download a map before your arrival. It's a little hard to find, so before you take off, check out the trail map on the back of the fee-station signboard. Three loops can be made—3.3, 3.7, and 4 miles—offering forests of the river-floodplain and piedmont types. The first trailhead is about 100 feet behind the fee-station signboard as you face it. The second trail-access point is harder to find—look for the painted blazes on the right side of the day-use area road, a little past the covered signboard in the picnic area. The blazes are on two side-by-side cedar trees. No matter whether it is land or water, fine Carolina recreation is at hand here at Woods Ferry.

Woods Ferry Campground

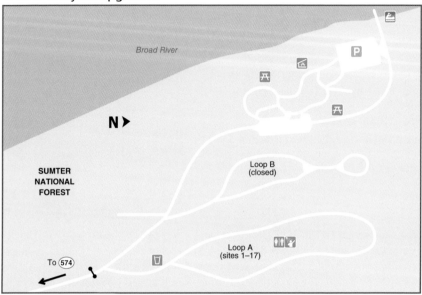

GETTING THERE

From Exit 74 on I-26 near Newberry, South Carolina, head northeast on SC 34 for 18.8 miles. Turn left on SC 215, and follow it 14.5 miles. Turn right on SC 121/SC 72, and follow it 1.4 miles. Turn left on Leeds Road, and follow it 2.1 miles. Veer left on Woods Ferry Road, crossing the railroad tracks, and go 3.6 miles. Turn left on Park Road/County Road 574, and follow it 3.6 miles to the campground.

GPS COORDINATES: N34° 41.981'   W81° 27.022'

SOUTH CAROLINA LOWCOUNTRY

The pier at Huntington Beach State Park *(see campground 49, page 161)*

48

⚠ Honey Hill Campground

Beauty ★★★ Privacy ★★★ Spaciousness ★★★ Quiet ★★★ Security ★★ Cleanliness ★★★

Honey Hill can be your headquarters for exploring the Lowcountry's Francis Marion National Forest.

This campground is nothing to climb a hill and shout about. However, it is one of the better tent-camping options in the Francis Marion National Forest. The forest is named for the Revolutionary War General Francis Marion, nicknamed the Swamp Fox. The forest is an underutilized treasure of South Carolina, where adventurers can hike and/or bike the Palmetto Trail at its very beginning and explore tidally influenced waterways just a few miles from the Atlantic Ocean. Consider the campground a way station for exploring, as opposed to an end destination in and of itself.

Honey Hill is only 32 feet high in elevation, but a little height here in the Lowcountry can mean a lot. The elevation gain from nearby McClellanville to Honey Hill is nearly imperceptible. A fire tower stands next to the campground, though, unfortunately, it is

Paddlers float through Wambaw Creek Wilderness.

KEY INFORMATION

CONTACT: Francis Marion Ranger District, Francis Marion National Forest, 843-336-3248; www.fs.usda.gov/scnfs

OPEN: Year-round

SITES: 8

EACH SITE HAS: Picnic table, grill

WHEELCHAIR ACCESS: Yes

ASSIGNMENT: First come, first served; no reservations

REGISTRATION: Self-registration

AMENITIES: Water spigot, vault toilet

PARKING: At campsites only

FEE: None

ELEVATION: 32'

RESTRICTIONS:

PETS: On leash only

FIRES: In fire grates only

ALCOHOL: At campsites only

OTHER: 14-day stay limit

retired. Pass the tower and enter a gravel loop. Live oaks, hickories, sweet gums, and pines shade the campground. Spanish moss hangs from the trees. Grass grows where the sun shines. The campground is a little on the unkempt side, as in sites not being numbered or exactly delineated.

All the campsites are on the outside of the loop. The first site is somewhat open and grassy. Loop around past well-separated camps. The final two sites are large and shady and back up to Forest Service Road 219. The center of the loop has an information kiosk and a pump well. A vault toilet is at the loop's beginning. During the warm season, mosquitoes can be troublesome in the Francis Marion National Forest. The elevation of Honey Hill keeps it drier and less buggy than other campgrounds. Smart forest visitors will call ahead for a bug report and plan their recreation activities during the cooler months. A great time to visit is in fall after the first frost. The forest offers plenty of autumn color to enjoy.

A Francis Marion National Forest map is a must for getting around. Order one before you arrive, or stop at the Sewee Visitor Center on US 17 in Awendaw. The visitor center has trails of its own, informative displays, and programs. It pays to call ahead for hiking and paddling information about the forest. Four national forest wilderness areas are just a few miles from Honey Hill. Intrepid adventurers can see all four, but Wambaw Creek Wilderness is easily the most accessible. Take a 6.6-mile canoe trip from Still Landing to

Pitcher plants on the Swamp Fox Passage of the Palmetto Trail

Echaw Road along a blackwater creek flanked by tupelo and cypress trees. This is Palmetto State paddling at its finest.

Little Wambaw Swamp Wilderness is very primitive. Explorers can follow old built-up tram roads amid swampland. The only catch is that the tram bridges have eroded away, leaving wading a certainty. This wilderness has even less dry ground in its 4,815 acres. This swamp is reportedly the least-visited locale in the whole state. Hellhole Bay Wilderness has a 5-mile channel that can be paddled during high water. Call ahead about water levels. Nearby Echaw Creek offers first-rate paddling in a nonwilderness setting and is much more user-friendly. Start at Pitch Landing and paddle down intimate Echaw Creek to reach the wide Santee River after 3 miles. Head down the Santee River 2 more miles to McConnell's Landing.

The Palmetto Trail, South Carolina's master path, begins its journey to the Upcountry here in the Francis Marion National Forest. This part of the trail was formerly known as the Swamp Fox Trail. It starts near Buck Hall Campground and heads along Awendaw Creek toward the interior to Halfway Creek and beyond, 27 miles to the Witherbee Ranger Station. From there it is 15 more miles to Lake Moultrie. Visit palmettoconservation.org for more information on the Palmetto Trail. Then leave the virtual world behind and see the real thing here at Honey Hill in the Francis Marion National Forest.

Honey Hill Campground

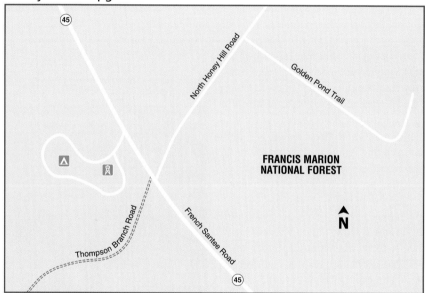

GETTING THERE

From the intersection of US 17 and SC 41 in Mount Pleasant, South Carolina, just northeast of Charleston, head northeast on US 17, and go 25.9 miles. Turn left on SC 45, and go 8.2 miles to the campground, on your left.

GPS COORDINATES: N33° 10.468'   W79° 33.707'

49

Huntington Beach State Park Campground

Beauty ★★★ Privacy ★★★ Spaciousness ★★★ Quiet ★★★★ Security ★★★★★ Cleanliness ★★★

This oceanside park is close—but not too close—to Myrtle Beach.

Campers come to Huntington Beach for a variety of reasons. Many enjoy the beach and other natural aspects of this 2,500-acre preserve in a fast-developing coast. Others relax in the campground after seeking activities outside the park. Either way, they enjoy this get-away, one of the limited public-beach camping locales in South Carolina near Myrtle Beach.

The North Campground, a short walk from the beach, has two large loops with a separate walk-in tent-camping area. The first loop has the sites closest to the beach, in a mix of sun and shade from planted cedars and live oaks. This is the land of the RV, but there are some good sites here. Make reservations for odd-numbered sites 1–31 in this loop. A recreation building, near site 19, is convenient for getting out of those inevitable summer thunderstorms. Avoid sites 74–88 and 90–102, which are located on crossroads within the loop. Most sites on the remainder of the first loop have at least one shade tree. (Woe to

The shoreline at Huntington Beach

KEY INFORMATION

CONTACT: 843-237-4440;
southcarolinaparks.com/huntington-beach

OPEN: Year-round

SITES: 6 walk-in, 131 others, 42 full hook-up

EACH SITE HAS: Walk-ins have tent pad, picnic table, and fire ring; others have electricity and water (66 also have sewer)

WHEELCHAIR ACCESS: Yes

ASSIGNMENT: First come, first served and by reservation (866-345-7275; reserve.south carolinaparks.com/huntington-beach)

REGISTRATION: At office–gift shop

AMENITIES: Hot showers, water spigots, flush toilets, Wi-Fi

PARKING: At walk-in-camper parking area and at campsites only; 2 vehicles/site

FEE: $17–$35 walk-ins; $21–$62 others, depending on season

ELEVATION: Sea level

RESTRICTIONS:

PETS: On 6' or shorter leash only

FIRES: In fire rings only

ALCOHOL: Prohibited

OTHER: 6 people and 2 tents/site; 14-day stay limit in peak season; 30'–40' RV-length limit; quiet hours 10 p.m.–7 a.m.; fireworks prohibited

those stuck in a sunny site on a hot South Carolina summer day.) The second loop has the sites farthest from the ocean. Many of them have thick brush between sites, offering good privacy but little overhead shade.

Try to get one of the walk-in tent sites if you can; they are first come, first served. To reach them, leave the walk-in parking area and follow a sandy trail past a water spigot. Site T-1 lies beneath a large live oak. T-2 is more open. T-3 is shaded by pines and live oaks. T-4 is rather small. T-5 is large and well shaded. T-6 is the farthest back and set amid privacy-giving brush.

This popular state park fills weekends from March to September and many weekdays during the peak of summer. Many sites can be reserved, especially those closest to the beach. These beachside sites are often filled with RVs—location has its price, but proximity to an ocean breeze will cut down on insects when they are bothersome (usually following rainy periods). The walk-in tent sites offer much more privacy and the experience tent campers are after. A camp store is conveniently located inside the park.

The South Campground, opened in 2018, caters to people with RVs, as all 42 sites offer full hook-ups. In addition to the prevalence of RVs in this section, the sites are very close together. The beachside sites offer more shade.

Huntington Beach State Park prides itself on its naturalist programs. Checking out the alligators on the park causeway is a popular pastime. Let park personnel inform you about these ancient creatures. Other programs cover birding, the salt marsh, seashells, whales, dolphins, and the historic homesite known as Atalaya. This winter home of park benefactors Collis and Anna Huntington is modeled after houses on the Spanish Mediterranean coast. Rangers lead tours of this home, and three different park programs are held during the busy season, March–September. The park education center offers more learning experiences.

Three miles of beachfront attract ocean enthusiasts who shell, surf fish, or just relax while listening to the waves roll in. I first came here more than two decades ago. A jetty at the north end of the beach is also a popular fishing spot. Some folks will hike the two nature trails or kayak the saltwater marsh. But many others will enjoy the attractions of the nearby tourist destinations at Myrtle Beach, ranging from miniature golf to dinner shows to waterslides. Shoppers will look for the perfect grass basket from the area or a hammock from Pawleys Island. So whether you prefer to shop and act the part of the hokey tourist or to just enjoy the undeveloped shoreline, Huntington Beach may be the place for you.

Huntington Beach State Park Campgrounds

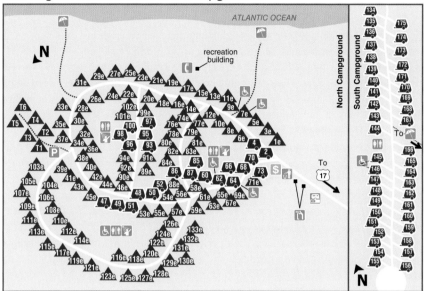

GETTING THERE

From the intersection of US 501 and US 17 in Myrtle Beach, South Carolina, take US 17 south 16.9 miles to the state park, on your left. Turn left into the park, and go about 1 mile to reach the campground. The park's address is 16148 Ocean Highway, Murrells Inlet, SC 29576.

GPS COORDINATES: N33° 30.370'   W79° 03.840'

50

Little Pee Dee State Park Campground

Beauty ★★★ Privacy ★★★ Spaciousness ★★★★ Quiet ★★★★ Security ★★★★★ Cleanliness ★★★★

Time slows down at this backwater state park.

Little Pee Dee State Park is one of those destinations that time seems to have passed by. The park exudes an atmosphere as slow moving as the Little Pee Dee River, for which it is named. I drove in during a weekday and barely saw a soul, other than a ranger who rolled by after I set up camp. After registering me, he confirmed that the park is indeed as relaxing and forgotten as it appears. In his 12 years there, he had seen the 50-site campground fill only twice. Many of the campers who do visit are folks from the Myrtle Beach area who want to escape the madness that sometimes envelops that tourist destination.

The campground is laid out in a grand loop along the shores of Lake Norton. The sandy road leads to sand parking spurs. Many pines and oaks grow overhead, while dogwoods are a prevalent understory tree. Oddly, the first two campsites in the loop are 49 and 50. Then the numbering becomes more conventional. Two small subloops spur from the main loop. Curve toward the lake, passing a picnic area with a covered shelter near site 7 and pass some lakeside sites. Large and well separated from each other, these sites have raked-sand floors, with needles and oak leaves marking their perimeter. Because the campground rarely gets crowded, you likely won't have a neighbor at the campsite next door, so privacy isn't much of an issue.

Taking a break at a sandbar on the Little Pee Dee River

KEY INFORMATION

CONTACT: 843-774-8872;
southcarolinaparks.com/little-pee-dee

OPEN: Year-round

SITES: 5 tent-only, 45 others

EACH SITE HAS: Tent sites have picnic
tables, fire rings, and water; others also
have electricity

WHEELCHAIR ACCESS: Yes

ASSIGNMENT: First come, first served and by
reservation (866-345-7275; reserve.south
carolinaparks.com/little-pee-dee)

REGISTRATION: Ranger will come by to
register you

AMENITIES: Hot showers, water, flush toilets

PARKING: At campsites only

FEE: $9–$11 tent-only; $16–$20 others

ELEVATION: 100'

RESTRICTIONS:

PETS: On 6' or shorter leash only

FIRES: In fire rings only

ALCOHOL: Prohibited

OTHER: 14-day stay limit

The subloop curves away from the lake and joins the main loop; lakeside sites resume with site 20. The next few sites, which offer great vistas of Lake Norton, are the campground's most coveted. Leaving the lake again, the official tent sites start with site 33. Because they are nonelectric, they are cheaper and in less demand than the electric sites.

I stayed in site 34 and was the only tent camper that night, warmed by a piney fire. A front moved in later, further warming the air and bringing rain. Breaking camp in the rain is never fun, but it's a fact of tent camping if you do it often enough.

The Beaver Pond Nature Trail begins just past site 40. This is more of a leg-stretching path than a bona fide hiking trail, though it does loop to a beaver pond. The tent sites here have thicker woods around them, are less used, and angle ever so slightly downhill toward Lake Norton. Complete the loop near some very large tent sites suitable for a family gathering. At the center of the loop are two bathhouses, the newer of which is heated, a fact I appreciated during my late-fall trip. A play area is also in the loop's center.

This part of South Carolina, Dillon County, is rural and relaxing. Little Pee Dee's 835 acres, stretched along the Little Pee Dee River, mark the apex of this quietness. A park lake, adding more aquatic beauty, complements the river and adjoining swamp. The damming of Bell Swamp Branch and Indian Pot Branch forms Lake Norton. The 54-acre impoundment, breached in 2016 due to Hurricane Matthew but later repaired, is a no-gas-motors lake, keeping the atmosphere serene. It does have a boat launch, however, and offers boat rentals for those who want to tour the lake or do some freshwater fishing. Anglers can also fish from the banks of the lake or from the nearby lake dam.

The park's namesake is also a boating possibility. The Little Pee Dee is a fine example of a coastal-plain blackwater river. Cypress trees and tupelo line much of it, as do sandbars, which are great for picnicking or relaxing. The river is tough to access from the park bridge but boasts landings and accesses nearby. Instead of trying to figure out all the particulars of a canoe trip, though, why not leave it to the outfitters? Betwixt the Rivers, based in nearby Marion, South Carolina, offers trips of varying lengths. Reach them at 843-423-1919. Make sure you have a little extra time on your hands, as life is slow and relaxing in this part of the Palmetto State.

Little Pee Dee State Park Campground

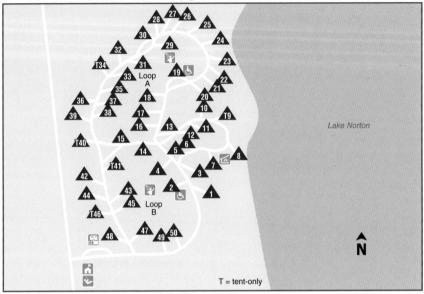

Lake Norton

T = tent-only

N

GETTING THERE

From Exit 190 on I-95 near Dillon, South Carolina, head east on SC 34. Go 2.3 miles, and continue on SC 57/SC 9. Go 6.6 miles, and turn right on State Park Road. Follow it 4 miles to the state park entrance, on your left. Enter the park, and go 1.2 miles to reach the campground. The park's address is 1298 State Park Road, Dillon, SC 29536.

GPS COORDINATES: N34° 19.682'   W79° 15.804'

APPENDIX A

CAMPING EQUIPMENT CHECKLIST

Except for the large and bulky items on this list, I keep a plastic storage container full of the essentials of car camping so that they're ready to go when I am. I make a last-minute check of the inventory, resupply anything that's low or missing, and away I go!

COOKING UTENSILS
Bottle opener
Bottles of salt, pepper, spices, and sugar
Can opener
Cooking oil and maple syrup in waterproof, spill-proof containers
Corkscrew
Cups, plastic or tin
Dish soap (biodegradable), sponge, towel
Fire starter
Flatware
Food of your choice
Frying pan, spatula
Fuel for stove
Lighter, matches in waterproof container
Plates
Pocketknife
Pot with lid
Stove
Tinfoil
Wooden spoon

FIRST AID KIT
See page 4.

SLEEPING GEAR
Pillow
Sleeping bag
Sleeping pad, inflatable or insulated
Tent with ground sheet and rainfly

MISCELLANEOUS
Bath soap (biodegradable), washcloth, and towel
Camp chair
Candles
Cooler
Deck of cards
Flashlight or headlamp
Lantern
Maps (road, trail, topographic, and the like)
Paper towels
Sunglasses
Toilet paper
Water bottle
Weather radio
Wool blanket
Zip-top plastic bags

OPTIONAL
Barbecue grill
Binoculars
Field guides on bird, plant, and wildlife identification
Fishing rod and tackle
Hatchet

APPENDIX B

SOURCES OF INFORMATION

The following is a partial list of agencies, associations, and organizations to contact for information on outdoor recreation opportunities in the Carolinas.

NORTH CAROLINA

Blue Ridge Parkway
828-271-4779
nps.gov/blri

Great Smoky Mountains National Park
865-436-1200
nps.gov/grsm

National Forests in North Carolina
828-257-4200
www.fs.usda.gov/nfsnc

North Carolina Department of Tourism
800-VISIT-NC (847-4862)
visitnc.com

North Carolina State Parks
919-707-9300
ncparks.gov

SOUTH CAROLINA

Francis Marion and Sumter National Forests
828-257-4200
www.fs.usda.gov/scnfs

Kings Mountain National Military Park
864-936-7921
nps.gov/kimo

South Carolina Department of Tourism
803-734-1062
discoversouthcarolina.com

South Carolina State Parks
803-734-0156
southcarolinaparks.com

U.S. Army Corps of Engineers
Savannah District
800-533-3478
www.sas.usace.army.mil

INDEX

Check out these great titles from
Adventure Publications!

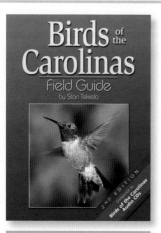

Birds of the Carolinas Field Guide

By Stan Tekiela
ISBN: 978-1-59193-066-2
$14.95, 1st Edition
4.38 x 6, paperback
368 pages
Color photographs

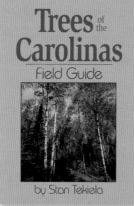

Trees of the Carolinas Field Guide

By Stan Tekiela
ISBN: 978-1-59193-199-7
$14.95, 1st Edition
4.38 x 6, paperback
332 pages
Color photographs

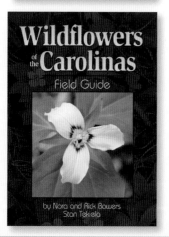

Wildflowers of the Carolinas Field Guide

By Nora and Rick Bowers and
    Stan Tekiela
ISBN: 978-1-59193-195-9
$16.95, 1st Edition
4.38 x 6, paperback
430 pages
Color photographs

Check out this great title from
Menasha Ridge Press!

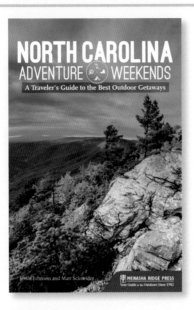

North Carolina Adventure Weekends

by Jessie Johnson & Matt Schneider
ISBN: 978-1-63404-092-1
$16.95, 1st Edition

5.5 x 8.5, paperback
Full color, 216 pages
Maps, photographs, index

North Carolina Adventure Weekends takes readers to the best destinations in North Carolina for 48 hours of maximum adventure. Whether you're a novice or an experienced adventurer, North Carolina offers a variety of outdoor pursuits to enjoy—from camping in Pisgah National Forest to canoeing down the Nantahala River and hiking in the Croatan National Forest. There's no need to spend hours researching the best destinations or go on long, expensive trips. This book is for hikers who love to climb, paddlers who love to pedal, and anyone else whose idea of unwinding is an action-packed weekend in the great outdoors. With 12 exciting trips to choose from, you'll know where to stay and which adventures are truly weekend-worthy.

Each chapter in this full-color guide highlights a focused geographic area and includes detailed directions, so readers can spend more time playing and less time driving from place to place. Adventurers will also learn where to stock up on supplies, what to do on a rainy day, and where to go to rehash the weekend's adventures over an epic-worthy meal and a beer.

  **MENASHA RIDGE PRESS**
www.menasharidge.com

Check out this great title from
Menasha Ridge Press!

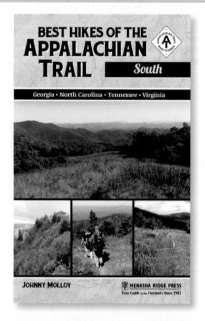

Best Hikes of the Appalachian Trail: South

by Johnny Molloy
ISBN: 978-0-89732-474-8
$17.95, 1st Edition

5x8, paperback
288 pages
Maps, photographs, index

Best Hikes of the Appalachian Trail: South takes readers directly to the best experiences to be had on the Appalachian Trail in the South. The book details 45 hikes along the AT, from the trail's southern terminus atop Springer Mountain in Georgia, north through North Carolina and Tennessee, and on into Virginia to the Maryland state line. These hikes will take you to overlooks, waterfalls, and wildernesses, as well as scenic, cultural, and historical sites, and even trail towns.

Using veteran outdoor writer Johnny Molloy's three decades of experience exploring the Southern Appalachians, this book is a true compilation of the best hikes on the Appalachian Trail in the South.

MENASHA RIDGE PRESS
www.menasharidge.com

ABOUT THE AUTHOR

Johnny Molloy is an outdoors writer based in Johnson City, Tennessee. Born in Memphis, he moved to Knoxville in 1980 to attend the University of Tennessee. It was in Knoxville that he developed his love of the natural world, which has since become the primary focus of his life.

photographed by Keri Anne Molloy

It all started on a backpacking foray into Great Smoky Mountains National Park.

That first trip, though a disaster, unleashed an innate love of the outdoors that has led to his spending more than 150 nights per year, over the past 25 years, tent camping, backpacking, and canoe camping throughout the United States and abroad. In 1987, after graduating from the University of Tennessee with a degree in economics, he continued to spend an ever-increasing amount of time in natural places, becoming more skilled in a variety of environments. Friends enjoyed his adventure stories; one even suggested he write a book. Soon he parlayed his love of the outdoors into an occupation.

His efforts have resulted in almost 80 books, ranging from hiking guides to paddling guides to camping guides and to true outdoor-adventure stories. His books have covered all or part of 26 states, primarily in the East. Johnny's Carolina books include *Top Trails: Great Smoky Mountains National Park; Hiking North Carolina's National Forests; 50 Hikes in South Carolina; Best Easy Day Hikes Charleston, South Carolina;* and *Paddling South Carolina.*

Johnny has also written numerous articles for magazines and websites. He continues to write and travel extensively to all four corners of the United States, pursuing a variety of outdoor interests. For the latest information about the author, visit johnnymolloy.com.

DEAR CUSTOMERS AND FRIENDS,

SUPPORTING YOUR INTEREST IN OUTDOOR ADVENTURE, travel, and an active lifestyle is central to our operations, from the authors we choose to the locations we detail to the way we design our books. Menasha Ridge Press was incorporated in 1982 by a group of veteran outdoorsmen and professional outfitters. For many years now, we've specialized in creating books that benefit the outdoors enthusiast.

Almost immediately, Menasha Ridge Press earned a reputation for revolutionizing outdoors- and travel-guidebook publishing. For such activities as canoeing, kayaking, hiking, backpacking, and mountain biking, we established new standards of quality that transformed the whole genre, resulting in outdoor-recreation guides of great sophistication and solid content. Menasha Ridge Press continues to be outdoor publishing's greatest innovator.

The folks at Menasha Ridge Press are as at home on a whitewater river or mountain trail as they are editing a manuscript. The books we build for you are the best they can be, because we're responding to your needs. Plus, we use and depend on them ourselves.

We look forward to seeing you on the river or the trail. If you'd like to contact us directly, visit us at menasharidge.com. We thank you for your interest in our books and the natural world around us all.

SAFE TRAVELS,

Bob Sehlinger

BOB SEHLINGER
PUBLISHER